NEW YORK

P9-CQI-512

NATIONAL GEOGRAPHIC

FIELD GUIDE TO

BIRDS

NEW YORK

NATIONAL GEOGRAPHIC

FIELD GUIDE TO

BIRDS

Edited by JONATHAN ALDERFER

National Geographic
Washington, D.C.

N ew York's varied topography and myriad habitats make for exciting and unpredictable birding almost any day of the year. From the Adirondacks' peaks towering above tree line, to the massive freshwater wetland complex at Montezuma National Wildlife Refuge, to the coastal scrub thickets of Long Island, the state boasts a multitude of habitats. With approximately 460 species on its official list, New York offers a sizable cross section of North America's birds.

Large expanses of unbroken forest remain. While much land is still developed for agriculture, an increasing amount is reverting to mature forest. As a result, New York is one of the best places in the United States to find breeding wood warblers: Up to 33 of the 54 North American breeders nest there! Overall, at least 254 species of birds have bred in New York, a testament to its complex and varied habitat.

One of New York's finest treasures is its array of migration hot spots. The entire Long Island coast is a "migrant trap" in autumn, where on blustery days the low, coastal vegetation can abound with landbirds while migrant raptors move south overhead. New York City's Central Park is a fine place to see migrants in both spring and fall. The south shore of Lake Ontario offers stellar opportunities to witness spring migrants. At Derby Hill and Braddock Bay more than 100,000 raptors have been counted in a single season! In mid-April when a strong south wind is blowing, grab your binoculars and head to either of those locations to find huge numbers of Broad-winged Hawks circling overhead, while hundreds of other raptors move north along the lake shore.

New York is indeed a great state for birding, and we invite you to experience it to its fullest.

BRIAN SULLIVAN
Cornell Lab of Ornithology
Ithaca, NY

FRONTISPIECE: HOODED MERGANSER
PHOTO BY ROBERT ROYSE

CONTENTS

SELECTED BIRDING SITES OF
NEW YORK

ONTARIO

miles

0   50   100

0   50   100
kilometers

Thousand Islands

Point
Peninsula
Watertown

LAKE ONTARIO

Derby Hill
Bird Observatory

HAMLIN BEACH
S.P.   Braddock
              Bay
                    Greece
TUSCARORA I.R.   Lockport   Erie Canal   Irondequoit   Oneida
                                IROQUOIS   Lake
Niagara Falls   N.W.R.   Gates   Oswego
Niagara Falls   Tonawanda   Niagara Falls   TONAWANDA I.R.   Rochester   Onondaga Lake
          Amherst   MONTEZUMA N.W.R.   Syracuse
Buffalo   Cheektowaga   Auburn   ONONDAGA
    Tifft   W. Seneca   Canandaigua   L.   I.R.
L. ERIE   Nature   Finger Lakes   Cayuga
CANADA   Preserve   CATTARAUGUS   L.
U.S.   I.R.   Keuka   Seneca L.   FINGER LAKES
                            Lake   N.F.   Ithaca
          Cattaraugus Cr.   Chemung
Ripley   OIL   Genesee
Hawkwatch   SPRINGS
Chautauqua L.   I.R.
                    ALLEGANY   Elmira   Binghamton
Jamestown   I.R.
              ALLEGANY
              STATE PARK

Allegheny   P E N N S Y L V A N I A

MAP KEY

□ National Park, N.P.
  National Monument, NAT. MON.
  National Recreation Area, N.R.A.

  National Forest, N.F.

□ National Wildlife Refuge, N.W.R.

□ State Park, S.P.

  Indian Reservation

···· International boundary

▦▦▦ State boundary

- -   Trail

───   National wild & scenic river

╱   Dam

⊛   State capital

□   Point of interest

LOOKING AT BIRDS

W hat do the artist and the nature lover share? A passion for being attuned to the world and all of its complexity, via the senses. Every time you go out into the natural world, or even view it through a window, you have another opportunity to see what is there. And the more you know what you are looking at, the more you see.

Even if you are not yet a committed birder, it makes sense to take a field guide with you when you go out for a walk or a hike. Looking for and identifying birds will sharpen and heighten your perceptions, and intensify your experience. And you'll find that you notice everything else more acutely—the terrain, the season, the weather, the plant life, other animal life.

Birds are beautiful, complex animals that live everywhere around us in our towns and cities and in distant places we dream of visiting. Here in North America more than 900 species have been recorded—from abundant commoners to the rare and exotic. A comprehensive field reference like the *National Geographic Field Guide to the Birds of North America* is essential for understanding that big picture. If you are taking a spring walk in the Catskills, however, you may want something simpler: a guide to the birds you are most likely to see, which slips easily into a pocket.

This photographic guide is designed to provide an introduction to the common birds—and some of the specialty birds—you might encounter in New York: how to identify them, how they behave, and where to find them, with specific locations.

Discovery, observation, and identification of birds is exciting, whether you are novice or expert. I know that every time I go out to look at birds, I see more clearly and have a greater appreciation for the natural world and my own place in it.

JONATHAN ALDERFER
Editor

National Geographic Field Guide to Birds: New York is designed to help beginning and practiced birders alike identify birds in the field and introduce them to the region's varied birdlife. The book is organized by bird families, following the order in the *Check-list of North American Birds,* by the American Ornithologists' Union. Families share structural characteristics, and by learning these shared characteristics early, birders can establish a basis for a lifetime of identifying birds and related family members with great accuracy—sometimes merely at a glance. (For quick reference in the field, use the color and alphabetical indexes at the back of this book.)

A family may have one member or dozens of members, or species. In this book each family is identified by its common name in English along the right-hand border of each spread. Each species is also identified in English, with its Latin genus and species—its scientific name—found directly underneath. One species is featured in each entry.

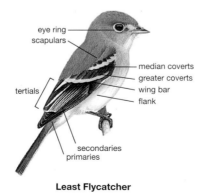

eye ring
scapulars

median coverts
greater coverts
wing bar
flank

tertials

secondaries
primaries

Least Flycatcher

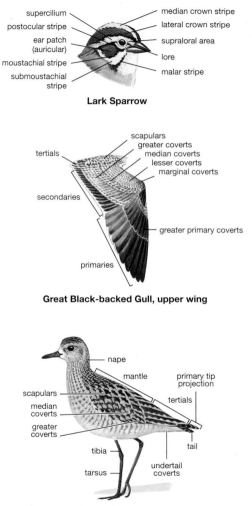

Lark Sparrow

supercilium
postocular stripe
ear patch (auricular)
moustachial stripe
submoustachial stripe

median crown stripe
lateral crown stripe
supraloral area
lore
malar stripe

Great Black-backed Gull, upper wing

scapulars
greater coverts
median coverts
lesser coverts
marginal coverts

tertials

secondaries

greater primary coverts

primaries

Pacific Golden-Plover

nape

mantle

primary tip projection

scapulars
median coverts
greater coverts

tertials

tibia

tarsus

undertail coverts

tail

An entry begins with **Field Marks**, the physical clues used to quickly identify a bird, such as body shape and size, bill length, and plumage color or pattern. A bird's body parts yield vital clues to identification, so a birder needs to become familiar with them early on. After the first glance at body type, take note of the head shape and markings, such as stripes, eye rings, and crown markings. Bill shape and color are important as well. Note body and wing details: wing bars, color of and pattern of wing feathers at rest, and shape and markings when extended in flight. Tail shape, length, color, and banding may play a big part, too. At left are diagrams detailing the various parts of a bird— its topography—labeled with the term likely to be found in the text of this book.

The main body of each entry is divided into three categories: Behavior, Habitat, and Local Sites. The **Behavior** section details certain characteristics to look or listen for in the field. Often a bird's behavioral characteristics are very closely related to its body type and field marks, such as in the case of woodpeckers, whose stiff tails, strong legs, and sharp claws enable them to spend most of their lives in an upright position, braced against a tree trunk. The **Habitat** section describes areas that are most likely to support the featured species. Preferred nesting locations of breeding birds are also included in many cases. The **Local Sites** section recommends specific refuges or parks where the featured bird is likely to be found. A section called **Field Notes** finishes each entry, and includes information such as plumage variations within a species; or it may introduce another species with which the featured bird is frequently confused. In either case, an additional drawing may be included to aid in identification.

Finally, a caption under each of the photographs gives the season of the plumage pictured, as well as the age and sex of the bird, if discernable. A key to using this informative guide and its range maps follows on the next two pages.

READING THE SPREAD

The labeled spread shows a field guide entry for:

CHESTNUT-SIDED WARBLER 197

Dendroica pensylvanica L 5" (13 cm)

FIELD MARKS
Breeding male has yellow crown; black eye and malar stripes; chestnut sides

Female has greenish crown and less chestnut

Two yellowish wing bars

Behavior
An active forager, often drooping its wings and cocking its tail above its back, gleans insects, caterpillars, seeds, and berries from low foliage or directly from ground. May sometimes take insects in flight. Nest of grass, sticks, and roots located near the ground in shrubby understory. Call is a loud, sweet *chip*. Male sings conspicuously from exposed perch a whistled *please, please, pleased to meetcha* or a *wee-wee-wee new preacher tree*.

Habitat
Breeds in open brushy woodlands, especially second-growth deciduous ones, and in overgrown fields. Found in a variety of woodlands during migration.

Local Sites
Lindsay-Parsons Biodiversity Preserve near Ithaca is a good place to look for breeding Chestnut-sided Warblers. They are also easily found as coastal migrants in September.

FIELD NOTES: During fall migration, which peaks in early September, immatures (inset) look very different. They are lime green above and whitish below, with a gray face and a distinct white eye ring. Adult males retain dull chestnut sides.

Breeding | Adult male

---

❶ Photograph: Shows bird in habitat. May be female or male, adult or juvenile. Plumage may be breeding, molting, nonbreeding, or year-round.

❷ Caption: Defines the featured bird's plumage, age, and sometimes sex, as seen in the picture.

❸ Heading: Beneath the common name find the Latin, or scientific, name. Beside it is the bird's length (L), and sometimes its wingspan (WS). Wingspan is given with birds often seen in flight. Female measurements are given if noticeably different from male.

❹ Field Marks: Gives basic facts for field identification: markings, head and bill shape, and body size.

❺ Band: Gives the common name of the bird's family.

❻ Range Map: Shows year-round range in purple, breeding range in red, winter range in blue. Areas through which species are likely to migrate are shown in green.

❼ Behavior: A step beyond **Field Marks**, gives clues to identifying a bird by its habits, such as feeding, flight pattern, courtship, nest-building, or songs and calls.

❽ Habitat: Reveals the area a species is most likely to inhabit, such as forests, marshes, grasslands, or urban areas. May include preferred nesting sites.

❾ Local Sites: Details local spots to look for the given species.

❿ Field Notes: A special entry that may give a unique point of identification, compare two species of the same family, compare two species from different families that are easily confused, or focus on a historical or conservation fact.

On each map of New York, range boundaries are drawn beyond which the species is not regularly seen. Nearly every species will be rare at the edges of its range. The sample map shown below explains the colors and symbols used on each map. Ranges continually expand and contract, so the map is a tool, not a rule. Range information is based on actual sightings and therefore depends upon the number of knowledgeable and active birders in each area.

Map Key

Breeding range, generally in spring and summer

Winter range

Year-round range

Migration range

Sample Map: Green-Winged Teal

READING THE INDEXES

There are two indexes at the back of this book. The first is a **Color Index** (p. 262), created to help birders quickly find an entry by noting its color in the field. In this index, male birds are labeled by their predominant color: Mostly White, Mostly Black, etc. Note that a bird may have a head of a different color than its label states. That's because its body—the part most noticeable in the field—is the color labeled.

The **Alphabetical Index** (p. 266) is organized by the bird's common name. Next to each entry is a check-off box. Most birders make lists of the birds they see. Some keep several lists, perhaps one of birds in a certain area and another of all the birds they've ever seen—a life list. Such lists enable birders to look back and remember their first sighting of an Indigo Bunting or an American Kestrel.

Year-round | Adult white morph

SNOW GOOSE

Chen caerulescens L 31" (79 cm) WS 56" (142 cm)

FIELD MARKS

White overall

Black primaries show in flight

Heavy pinkish bill with black "grinning patch"

Juvenile is dingy gray-brown on head, neck, and upperparts

Behavior

Travels in large flocks, especially during spring migration. Loud, vocal birds that sound like baying hounds, flocks migrate in loose V-formation and long lines, sometimes more than 1,500 miles nonstop, reaching speeds up to 40 mph. Primarily vegetarian, forages on agricultural grains and plants and aquatic vegetation. An agile swimmer, commonly rests on water during migration and at wintering grounds. Listen for its harsh, descending *whouk,* heard continuously in flight.

Habitat

Most often seen on grasslands, grainfields, and wetlands, favoring standing shallow freshwater marshes and flooded fields. Breeds in the Arctic.

Local Sites

The Snow Goose is common to abundant during spring and fall migrations in wetlands, especially along the coast in fall and at Montezuma National Wildlife Refuge in spring.

FIELD NOTES Amid a flock of white Snow Geese, you may see a few dark morphs as well, characterized by a varying amount of dark gray-brown on the back and breast (inset). These birds were formerly considered a separate species, the Blue Goose.

Year-round | Adult with downy young

CANADA GOOSE

Branta canadensis L 30-43" (75-108 cm) WS 59-73" (148-183 cm)

FIELD MARKS

Black head and neck marked with distinctive white chin strap

In flight, shows large, dark wings, white undertail coverts, and a long protruding neck

Brown body, paler below; white vent and belly

Behavior

A common, familiar goose; best known for migrating in large V-formation. Like some other members of its family, finds a mate and remains monogamous for life. Nests on the ground in open or forested areas near water. Its distinctive honking call makes it easy to identify, even without seeing it. Males give a lower-pitched *hwonk*, females a higher *hrink*.

Habitat

Prefers wetlands, grasslands, and cultivated fields within commuting distance of water. Has also adapted successfully to man-made habitats such as golf courses, landscaped ponds, and farms.

Local Sites

The Canada Goose is a common resident, found in the largest numbers in the lower Hudson Valley. Migrants are abundant throughout the state during spring and fall.

FIELD NOTES The Brant, *Branta bernicla* (inset) is a small, stocky goose with a black head, neck, and breast, and a whitish patch on the sides of its neck. It is an abundant migrant, and tens of thousands winter on the southern shore of Long Island.

Year-round | Adults

TUNDRA SWAN

Cygnus columbianus L 52" (132 cm)

FIELD MARKS
White overall

Black, slightly concave bill with yellow spot of variable size in front of eye

Juvenile appears darker with pinkish bill

Behavior
Feeds on aquatic vegetation in shallow water, its long neck enabling it to keep its body upright. Flies in straight lines or in V-formation, with its neck protruding forward. Using the same routes every year, the Tundra Swan migrates thousands of miles between Arctic breeding grounds and temperate wintering quarters. Call is a noisy, barking *kwooo*, often heard at night.

Habitat
Winters south of New York in coastal areas on ponds, lakes, estuaries, and marshes. Breeds on ponds in Alaska and the Arctic.

Local Sites
Tundra Swans are most easily seen during spring migration at Iroquois and Montezuma National Wildlife Refuges, though in recent winters up to 500 have remained at the north end of Cayuga Lake.

FIELD NOTES The introduced Mute Swan, *Cygnus olor* (inset: juvenile, left; adult, right), has a black knob at the base of an orange bill. At rest, the Mute Swan holds its neck in an S-curve, bill pointed down; the Tundra Swan's neck is straight. Mute Swans are increasing throughout New York state.

Breeding | Adult male

WOOD DUCK

Aix sponsa L 18.5" (47 cm)

FIELD MARKS
Male has glossy iridescent head and crest, lined in white; red, white, black, and yellow bill; burgundy breast with white spotting; yellowish sides

Female duller overall with large white teardrop-shaped eye patch

Behavior
Most commonly feeds by picking insects from the water's surface or by tipping into shallows to pluck invertebrates from the bottom, but may also be seen foraging on land. The omnivorous Wood Duck's diet changes throughout the year depending upon available foods and its need for particular proteins or minerals during migration, breeding, and molting. Nests in tree cavities or man-made nest boxes. Male Wood Ducks give a soft, upslurred whistle when swimming. Female Wood Ducks have a distinctive rising, squealing flight call of *ooEEK*.

Habitat
Inhabits woodlands and forested swamps.

Local Sites
Wood Ducks breed commonly statewide and are easily found during fall migration, when the highest concentrations occur on the Finger Lakes and on Lake Ontario.

FIELD NOTES The Wood Duck female (inset) hatches up to 15 eggs in cavities high up in trees or nest boxes. Once hatched, the young must make a long jump to the water, sometimes 30 feet below. Protected by their downy plumage, they generally land safely.

Breeding | Adult male

AMERICAN WIGEON

Anas americana L 19" (48 cm)

FIELD MARKS

White cap and forehead on male; green patch extending back from eyes; white wing patch

Both sexes have large white patch on underwing

Rusty brown chest, flanks, and back; white belly; pointed tail

Behavior

Grazes in fields and was once considered an agricultural pest. Often feeds in shallow water with other duck species; has also been known to forage in deeper waters, and to steal food from diving ducks or coots. Flushes readily if disturbed. Tight flocks careen together impressively. Male's whistle is a three-note *whew-whew-whew;* female gives off a low, harsh quack.

Habitat

Found in various wetland habitats, ranging from marshes to lakes, bays, coastal estuaries, flooded fields, and even golf courses. The American Wigeon's shallow nest is built on dry land among tall weeds.

Local Sites

Although the American Wigeon breeds sparsely in the state, look for it during fall migration at Montezuma National Wildlife Refuge and along the coast, where concentrations can be spectacular.

FIELD NOTES The American Wigeon has also been called the Baldpate, a reference to the male's white forehead and cap. A close relative, the Eurasian Wigeon, *Anas penelope*, is a rare visitor to New York. The male Eurasian has a cream-colored cap on a rufous head; females of the two species are very similar.

Year-round | Male

AMERICAN BLACK DUCK

Anas rubripes L 23" (58 cm)

FIELD MARKS

Blackish brown body, paler on face and foreneck

In flight, white wing linings contrast sharply with dark body; violet speculum bordered in black

Male's bill is yellow, female's is dull green

Behavior

Feeds in shallow water, mostly on aquatic vegetation in winter and aquatic insects in summer. Female builds nest of plant material and downy feathers in a shallow depression on the ground. The female Black Duck gives a typical loud *QUACK*; the male's call is shorter and lower-pitched.

Habitat

Found in woodland lakes and streams and in coastal marshes, often in the company of Mallards (next page).

Local Sites

The American Black Duck population has declined over the last several decades, but it is easily found year-round at Montezuma National Wildlife Refuge and in coastal marshes.

FIELD NOTES The population of the American Black Duck seems to be losing ground due to increased deforestation and displacement by the highly adaptable Mallard, with which the Black Duck often hybridizes. The breeding male Mallard is easily set apart by his green hood and grayish body, but the female Mallard (inset) more closely resembles the Black Duck. Look for her warmer brown body, orange bill with dark center, and blue speculum upper wing patch bordered in white.

Breeding | Adult male

MALLARD

Anas platyrhynchos L 23" (58 cm)

FIELD MARKS

Male has metallic green head and neck; white collar; chestnut breast

Female mottled brown overall; orange bill marked with black

Both sexes have bright blue speculum bordered in white; white tail and underwings

Behavior

A dabbler, the Mallard feeds by "tipping up" in shallow water and plucking seeds, grasses, and invertebrates from the bottom, as well as insects from the water's surface. In courtship, the male pumps his head, dips his bill, and rears up in the water to exaggerate his size. A female signals consent by duplicating the male's head-pumping. Nests on the ground in concealing vegetation. The female is known for her loud, descending *QUACK*. The male's call is shorter, softer, less common.

Habitat

This widespread species occurs wherever shallow fresh water is found, from rural swamps to city ponds.

Local Sites

A common resident, look for Mallards on just about any lake or pond, although many individuals are domestic rather than wild birds.

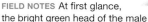

FIELD NOTES At first glance, the bright green head of the male Northern Shoveler, *Anas clypeata* (inset: female, left; male, right), can be mistaken for the Mallard's. Look for the Shoveler's large, dark, spatulate bill— a telltale mark on both sexes. The Northern Shoveler winters regularly in coastal areas.

Breeding | Adult male

NORTHERN PINTAIL

Anas acuta Male L 26" (66 cm) Female L 20" (51 cm)

FIELD MARKS

Male has chocolate brown head; long white neck stripes, breast, and underparts; gray back; long black central tail feathers

Female mottled brown overall

Long neck, slender body, and pointed tail evident in flight

Behavior

Often seen in small flocks during winter months, foraging for seeds in flooded agricultural fields or shallow ponds and marshes. Also eats aquatic insects, snails, beetles, and small crustaceans. This elegant duck is an accomplished flyer known for spilling out of the sky in spectacular rapid descents and leveling out directly into a landing. Male's call while breeding is a high, whining *mee-meee;* female utters a weak *quack.*

Habitat

Frequents both freshwater and saltwater marshes, ponds, lakes, and bays. Also found in flooded agricultural fields, especially during winter.

Local Sites

The Northern Pintail is a rare breeder in the state, but is easily found at Montezuma National Wildlife Refuge and at coastal marshes during spring and fall migrations.

FIELD NOTES The Northern Pintail female engages in an elaborate in-flight courtship ritual in which she veers, swerves, makes abrupt turns, and climbs, challenging her suitor to match her moves. If he succeeds, she rewards the male by allowing him to take her tail in his beak, or to pass below her so closely that their wing tips touch. If he fails her test, the female signals to another male to make an attempt.

Breeding | Adult male

GREEN-WINGED TEAL

Anas crecca L 14.5" (37 cm)

FIELD MARKS

Male's chestnut head has green ear patch

Female has mottled, dusky brown upperparts; white belly and undertail coverts

In flight, shows green speculum bordered above in buff

Behavior

Like other dabblers, the Green-winged Teal feeds at the water's surface or upended, tail in the air and head submerged, to reach aquatic plants, seeds, and invertebrates. An agile and fast flier, it travels in small flocks that twist and turn in midair. The Green-winged Teal migrates late, peaking in mid- to late October, and winters very far north—as far as Newfoundland—for such a small and cold-vulnerable duck. Nests are hidden in vegetation, within 200 feet of water. The female emits a high, thin *quack*; the male a sharp, whistled *kreek*.

Habitat

Found on shallow lakes and inland ponds, especially those with standing or floating vegetation. Also forages on mudflats.

Local Sites

The Green-winged Teal breeds at lakes and wetlands across the state, but it is most easily found during migration at Montezuma N.W.R.

FIELD NOTES In flight, wing patterns differ from those of the Blue-winged Teal, *Anas discors,* which is an uncommon breeder and common migrant in New York. The male Blue-winged Teal (inset) has a distinctive white crescent on his face, but the female is almost identical to the female Cinnamon Teal.

Breeding | Adult male

CANVASBACK

Aythya valisineria L 21" (53 cm)

FIELD MARKS

Male's head and neck are chestnut; back and sides whitish; breast and tail black

Female's head, neck, and breast are pale brown; back and sides pale gray

Forehead slopes to long, black bill

Behavior

Feeds on the water in large flocks, diving deep for fish, mollusks, and vegetation. Its heavy body requires a running start on water for takeoff. Flocks fly fairly high in lines or in irregular V-formation. Walks awkwardly, but not often seen on land. Both sexes are generally silent.

Habitat

Found in marshes, on lakes, and along large rivers. Breeds in thick marsh grasses on upper Great Plains and north through Canada to Alaska, where it is a frequent victim of brood parasitism by the closely related Redhead.

Local Sites

The Canvasback is outnumbered by Redheads on the Finger Lakes, but it is abundant during winter in coastal bays.

FIELD NOTES Sharing the male Canvasback's rufous head and neck, the male Redhead, *Aythya americana* (inset), can be difficult to distinguish in the field. Look for its grayer back, its tricolored bill of pale blue, white, and black, and for its yellow eyes—the Canvasback's eyes are red. The two species share much of the same range and nesting locations.

Breeding | Adult male

RING-NECKED DUCK

Aythya collaris L 17" (43 cm)

FIELD MARKS

Male has glossy purple head, breast, back, and tail; pale gray sides

Female is brown with pale face patch, eye ring, and eye stripe

Peaked crown; blue-gray bill with white ring and black tip

Behavior

An expert diver, the Ring-necked can feed on aquatic plants as deep as 40 feet below the water's surface, but tends to remain in shallower waters. Small flocks can be seen diving in shallow water for plants, roots, and seeds. Unlike most other diving ducks, the Ring-necked springs into flight directly from water, and flies in loose flocks with rapid wingbeats. Though often silent, the female sometimes gives a harsh, grating *deeer*.

Habitat

Fairly common in freshwater marshes and on woodland ponds and small lakes. Also found in marshes along large rivers in winter. Breeds across boreal forests of Canada and into the northern United States.

Local Sites

The Ring-necked Duck is encountered as a migrant more frequently in spring than in fall, but it is easily found at Montezuma National Wildlife Refuge during October. It is also common in winter along the coast.

FIELD NOTES The female Ring-necked Duck (inset) can be distinguished from plain, brown females of the two scaup species (p. 37) and the Redhead (p. 33) by her conspicuously banded bill, her prominent white eye ring, and her tall, peaked crown.

Breeding | Adult female, left; Adult male, right

GREATER SCAUP

Aythya marila L 18" (46 cm)

FIELD MARKS
Male has black head with green gloss; black neck, breast, and tail, a barred gray back, and white sides and belly

Female has dark brown upperparts, a white belly, and a bold white patch at base of bill

Behavior
Most often seen wintering in large, floating flocks. Dives down to 20 feet to feed on insects, mollusks, and aquatic vegetation, using its strong feet to propel itself underwater. Flies for the most part in straight lines with strong, rapid wingbeats. Though mostly silent, its eponymous call is a loud *scaup*.

Habitat
Found on large, open lakes and bays, and along shorelines. Prefers saltwater environments.

Local Sites
Look for the Greater Scaup during fall and winter on the bays of Long Island, where it is one of the most common duck species.

FIELD NOTES With nearly identical plumage on both sexes, the Lesser Scaup, *Aythya affinis* (inset: male, left; female, right), is best distinguished by its peaked crown; the Greater Scaup has a smoothly rounded head. Look also for the Lesser's shorter white wing stripe, which shows in flight. Another indicator is the Lesser's thinner, narrower bill, with a smaller black tip.

Breeding | Adult male

BUFFLEHEAD

Bucephala albeola L 13.5" (34 cm)

FIELD MARKS
Small duck with large puffy head, steep forehead, and short bill

Male has large white head patch and a glossy black back

Female is gray-brown overall with small, elongated white patches on either side of her head

Behavior
Often seen in small flocks, some birds keeping a lookout while others dive for aquatic insects, snails, and small fish. Like all diving ducks, its feet are set well back on its body to swiftly propel it through the water. Able to take off directly out of water, unlike many other diving ducks. Monogamous, Buffleheads are believed to stay with the same mate for years and to faithfully return to the same nesting site each season. Both sexes are generally silent away from the breeding grounds.

Habitat
Found on sheltered bays, rivers, and lakes in winter. Breeds primarily in Canada.

Local Sites
The Bufflehead is a common migrant and winter visitor on bays, rivers, and lakes throughout the state. Look for it especially on the back bays of Long Island in winter.

FIELD NOTES In winter, coastal bays and large lakes host the Long-tailed Duck, *Clangula hyemalis* (inset: male nonbreeding). Like the pintail (pages 28-9), it has a long tail visible in flight, but is set apart by a largely white back, a brown breast, and a stubby bill.

Breeding | Adult male

COMMON GOLDENEYE

Bucephala clangula L 18.5" (47 cm)

FIELD MARKS

Head black with greenish tinge on breeding male, brown on female

Male has white patches between eyes and bill; female has white neck ring and gray breast

Male is black above with white scapulars; female grayish above

Behavior

A diving duck; may be seen foraging in flocks, often with much of the flock diving simultaneously for aquatic insects, invertebrates, and plants. With feet located near its tail, the Common Goldeneye is an expert swimmer and diver, but walks very awkwardly on land. Male is generally silent outside of breeding grounds, but female occasionally gives a harsh, croaking *gack*. Listen as well for the low, stirring whistle made by the wings of the adult male in flight.

Habitat

Inhabits deep, open lakes and rivers near woodlands. In winter, also found in coastal areas. Look for this hardy duck even in open water between ice floes.

Local Sites

Though the Common Goldeneye breeds in the Adirondacks, it is found most easily during winter on the ocean off the east end of Long Island.

FIELD NOTES Distinctive marks to look for in the field on the female Common Goldeneye (inset) include her brown head, yellowish eye, mostly black bill with yellowish tip, and white neck ring. Both sexes show a large amount of white on their wings in flight.

Breeding | Adult male

HOODED MERGANSER

Lophodytes cucullatus L 18" (46 cm)

FIELD MARKS
Puffy, rounded crest

Male's white head patches are fan-shaped and conspicuous; black bill, back, and tail; white breast with two vertical black bars; chestnut sides

Female brownish gray overall with a rusty brown crest

Behavior
A diving duck; uses its wings and feet to propel itself underwater. Serrated bill is good for catching fish; also feeds on crustaceans, insects, and plants. Known at times to hunt cooperatively with other merganser species. Takes flight directly out of water, and moves swiftly with rapid wing beats. Though generally silent, throaty grunts and chatter can sometimes be heard from Hooded Mergansers. A displaying male will also emit a froglike growl.

Habitat
Winters on fresh and brackish water. In breeding season, found on woodland ponds, rivers, and back-waters, especially swamps.

Local Sites
One of New York's most widespread breeding ducks, the Hooded Merganser occurs on lakes and ponds throughout the state. In winter it favors freshwater lakes, primarily near the coast.

FIELD NOTES A distinctive field mark on the female Hooded Merganser (inset) is her thin, serrated bill with a dark upper mandible and a yellowish lower one. In flight, note both sexes' crests are flattened.

Breeding | Adult male

RED-BREASTED MERGANSER

Mergus serrator L 23" (58 cm)

FIELD MARKS

Male has a dark green head, a streaked breast, and a black back

Female has chestnut head, whitish chin and throat, and a gray-brown back

Both sexes have shaggy double crest and a red bill, hooked at tip

Behavior
Long, thin, serrated bill aids in catching small fish, the Red-breasted's principal food. Flaps wings and runs across water or land to take off, but once airborne is a strong, swift flyer, attaining speeds near 80 mph. A powerful swimmer, it uses its rear set feet to propel itself underwater. Often silent, the Red-breasted female may sometimes utter hoarse croaks.

Habitat
Typically winters along the coast, seeking sheltered bays, estuaries, and harbors that provide calm salt water in which to forage.

Local Sites
The Red-breasted Merganser is most easily found during migration and winter on Lake Ontario and the coast. It is also present in smaller numbers on the Finger Lakes.

FIELD NOTES The Common Merganser, *Mergus merganser* (inset, male) is larger than its Red-breasted relative, has whiter sides, and lacks a wispy crest. The dark head—green on the male and chestnut with a white chin on the female—is sharply defined from the white breast.

Year-round | Adult male

RING-NECKED PHEASANT

Phasianus colchicus Male L 33" (84 cm) Female L 21" (53 cm)

FIELD MARKS

Male iridescent bronze, mottled
with black, brown, and gray

Female buffy overall with dark
spotting and barring

Male has fleshy red face patches

Long tail; short, rounded wings

Behavior

An introduced Eurasian species, the Ring-necked
Pheasant feeds primarily on seeds and grain. Like
other game birds, it has a crop in which it stores food,
reducing the amount of time spent foraging in the
open. Tends to run rather than fly, but if flushed, rises
almost vertically with a loud whirring of its wings.
Nests on the ground in a shallow depression made by
the female. Male's territorial call is a loud, penetrating
kok-cack. Both sexes give hoarse, croaking alarm notes.

Habitat

Inhabits open country, farmlands, brushy areas, and
woodland edges.

Local Sites

Common statewide where it has been introduced as a
game bird. It occurs on the edges of fallow fields and
likes weedy hedgerows.

FIELD NOTES The Ring-necked Pheasant has been continually
reintroduced into different regions of North America since the
mid-1800s for hunting. First introduced into New York in the
1890s, populations of Ring-neckeds have been difficult to
maintain during the last 30 years due to new farming methods
and harsh winters of heavy snowfall. Introductions of different
subspecies from Asia have produced mixed stocks with
varying plumage.

Year-round | Adult gray morph

RUFFED GROUSE

Bonasa umbellus L 17" (43 cm)

FIELD MARKS
Grayish or redddish brown overall, mottled with white

Small crest; multibanded tail

Black ruff on neck, usually inconspicuous

Wide, dark band near tip of tail

Behavior
Forages on the ground primarily for seeds, nuts, fruit, and berries. Its diet varies by season, and may also include insects, amphibians, and small reptiles. If flushed, bursts into flight with a roar of its wings. Emits nasal squeals and clucks, especially when alarmed.

Habitat
A woodland bird which tends to remain in deciduous or mixed forests with brushy cover. May also be found near forest clearings.

Local Sites
The Ruffed Grouse is often heard before it is seen, giving its characteristic drumming from deep in the woods. It is a resident in mixed hardwood forests with scattered conifers.

FIELD NOTES The Ruffed Grouse is generally shy, elusive, and found singly, except in spring when the male (inset: gray morph) claims his territory and attracts females by raising his crest and neck ruff, fanning his tail and beating his wings rapidly, making a hollow, accelerating, drumming noise as he struts. This low-frequency noise is often said to be felt as much as heard.

Year-round | Adult male

WILD TURKEY

Meleagris gallopavo Male L 46" (117 cm) Female L 37" (94 cm)

FIELD MARKS

Large, with purple, green, and bronze iridescent plumage

Unfeathered blue and pink head with red wattles

Male has blackish breast tuft

Female smaller, less iridescent

Behavior

Largest of game birds, the turkey lives communally in small flocks. A ground feeder by day, the Wild Turkey roosts in trees at night. Forages for nuts, seeds, fruit, insects, frogs, and lizards. Flies well for short distances when alarmed, but prefers to walk or run. Females raise large broods, nesting in leaf-lined hollows in brush or woodlands. Male's characteristic display during breeding season involves puffing out his chest, swelling his wattles, spreading his tail, and rattling his wings, all while gobbling and strutting. In spring, the male's gobbling call may be heard from as far as a mile away.

Habitat

Frequents open forests, grainfields and forest edges.

Local Sites

The Wild Turkey is most easily seen at dawn and dusk wandering through farm fields, where it can be quite conspicuous in groups of 25 or more.

FIELD NOTES At the First Continental Congress held in Philadelphia in 1774, Benjamin Franklin argued for the turkey to be named the national bird, stating "He is besides, though a little vain & silly, a Bird of Courage, and would not hesitate to attack a Grenadier of the British Guards who should presume to invade his Farm Yard with a Red Coat on."

Nonbreeding | Adult

COMMON LOON

Gavia immer L 32" (81 cm)

FIELD MARKS

In winter: dark gray above, pale below; blue-gray bill; dark nape has white indentation each side

In spring and summer: back black-and-white checked; head dark green; neck striped; black bill

Behavior

A diving bird; eats fish up to 10 inches long, which it grasps with its pointed beak. Forages by diving and swimming underwater, propelled by large, paddle-shaped feet. Can stay submerged for up to three minutes at depths down to 250 feet. It is nearly impossible for the Common Loon to walk on land. Generally remains silent on wintering grounds.

Habitat

Winters in coastal waters, or inland on large lakes.

Local Sites

A rare breeder in the Adirondacks, the Common Loon is best found in winter on Lake Ontario, the Finger Lakes, and on the ocean and back bays of Long Island. Don't miss the spectacular migration of this species on Cayuga Lake, where hundreds can be observed in the fall.

FIELD NOTES The eponymous dark red throat patch of the Red-throated Loon, *Gavia stellata* (inset: nonbreeding), is visible only during breeding season. In winter, the Red-throated can be identified by the sharply defined white on its face, which extends farther back than that on the Common Loon, and by its habit of holding its thinner bill angled slightly upward.

Breeding | Adult

PIED-BILLED GREBE

Podilymbus podiceps L 13.5" (34 cm)

FIELD MARKS
Small and short-necked

Breeding adult brownish gray
overall; black ring around stout,
whitish bill; black chin and throat

Winter birds lose bill ring; chin
becomes white; plumage is
browner overall

Behavior
The most widespread of North American grebes, the
Pied-billed remains for the most part on water, seldom
on land or in flight. Dives for aquatic insects, small fish,
frogs, and vegetable matter. When alarmed, it slowly
sinks, holding only its head above the water's surface.
Like most grebes, the Pied-billed eats its own feathers
and feeds them to its young, perhaps to protect their
stomach linings from fish bones or animal shells. Song
is a series of slightly hollow, rapid-paced *kuh-kuh-kuh*s
or *k'owh-k'owh-k'owh*s.

Habitat
Prefers nesting around freshwater marshes and ponds.
Also found in more open waters of large bays and
rivers. Winters on both fresh and salt water.

Local Sites
The Pied-billed Grebe is easily observed in late summer
and fall at Montezuma National Wildlife Refuge, where
spectacular concentrations occur in early October.

FIELD NOTES The stark black-and-white
Horned Grebe, *Podiceps auritus* (inset: nonbreeding), is a common spring and fall migrant
throughout New York; it is also found in winter
on the coast and on inland lakes.

Breeding | Adult

DOUBLE-CRESTED CORMORANT

Phalacrocorax auritus L 32" (81 cm) WS 52" (132 cm)

FIELD MARKS

Black overall; facial skin yellow-orange; pale bill hooked at tip

Distinctive kinked neck in flight

Breeding adult has tufts of black feathers behind eyes

Immature has pale neck and breast

Behavior
In pursuit of prey, the Double-crested can dive to considerable depths, propelling itself with fully webbed feet. Uses its hooked bill to grasp fish. Feeds on a variety of aquatic life. May swim submerged to the neck, bill pointed slightly skyward. When it leaves the water, it perches on a branch, dock, or piling and half-spreads its wings to dry (pictured opposite). Soars at times, its neck in an S-shape. Nests near water either in trees or on rocks. Silent for the most part, but sometimes emits a deep grunt.

Habitat
Found along coasts, at inland lakes, and near rivers; it has adapted to fresh and saltwater environments.

Local Sites
The Double-crested Cormorant occurs throughout the state in summer and during migration, but in winter it is found only on Lake Ontario and at coastal locations. Best bets year-round are Lake Ontario and Long Island.

FIELD NOTES Despite its name, the crests on the head of the breeding Double-crested Cormorant are rarely seen in the field, especially in the case of the eastern breeding adult, whose crests are black and less conspicuous than the white crests of the western breeding adult. Juvenile birds are brownish above, and pale below, particularly on the breast and neck.

Breeding | Adult

GREAT BLUE HERON

Ardea herodias L 46" (117 cm) WS 72" (183 cm)

FIELD MARKS

Gray-blue overall; white foreneck
with black streaks; yellowish bill

Black stripe extends above eye

Breeding adult has plumes on its
head, neck, and back

Juvenile has dark crown; no plumes

Behavior

Waits for prey to come into its range, then spears it
with a quick thrust of its sharp bill. Eats almost any-
thing, from fish, reptiles, and amphibians, to rodents,
insects, and some small birds. Flies with its head folded
back onto its shoulders in an S-curve, typical of other
herons as well. When threatened, draws its neck back
with plumes erect and points its bill at antagonist. Pairs
build stick nests high in trees in loose association with
other Great Blue pairs. Mostly silent away from its nest,
but sometimes emits an annoyed, deep, guttural
kraaank as it takes flight.

Habitat

Hunts for aquatic creatures in marshes and swamps,
and for small mammals in fields and forest edges.

Local Sites

The hardy Great Blue Heron winters in coastal marshes
and, in warm years, north to the Finger Lakes region. It
breeds and migrates throughout the state and is easy to
find at almost any wet location during summer.

FIELD NOTES The generalist of the heron family, the Great Blue
feeds on fish, snakes, frogs, crabs, shrimp, and insects. Less
tied to aquatic habitats than other species, it will also give chase
to small birds, nestlings, or even small mammals, such as mice
and woodchucks, which it often wets before swallowing.

Breeding | Adult

GREAT EGRET

Ardea alba L 39" (99 cm) WS 51" (130 cm)

FIELD MARKS
Large white heron with heavy
yellow bill, black legs and feet

Breeding adult has long plumes
trailing from its back, extending
beyond the tail

Blue-green lores while breeding

Behavior
Stalks its prey slowly and methodically in shallow
water, uses its sharply pointed bill to capture small fish,
aquatic insects, frogs, and crayfish. Also known to hunt
snakes, birds, and small mammals. Occasionally forages
in groups or steals food from smaller birds. The Great
Egret makes its nest in trees or shrubs 10 to 40 feet
above the ground. Colonies may have as many as a
hundred birds. Generally silent except when nesting or
disturbed, when it may emit a guttural *kraak* or
repeated *cuk-cuk-cuk* notes.

Habitat
Inhabits both freshwater and saltwater wetlands.

Local Sites
Unlike the more southerly Snowy Egret, the Great Egret
breeds at several locations across the state. It is easily
found during summer on Long Island and at Montezuma National Wildlife Refuge.

FIELD NOTES Smaller than the Great Egret, the
Snowy Egret, *Egretta thula* (inset) is identified
by its thin, black bill, black legs, and bright yellow feet. It breeds commonly on Long Island,
and small numbers disperse inland after the
breeding season.

Year-round | Adult

GREEN HERON

Butorides virescens L 18" (46 cm) WS 26" (66 cm)

FIELD MARKS

Small, chunky heron with blue-green back and crown, sometimes raised to form shaggy crest

Back and sides of neck deep chestnut, throat white

Short yellow to orange legs

Behavior

Usually a solitary hunter, a Green Heron that lands near one of its kind is likely to be attacked. Stands motionless in or near water, waiting for a fish to come close enough for a swift attack. Spends most of its day in the shade, sometimes perched in trees or shrubs. When alarmed, it may make a show by flicking its tail, raising its crest, and elongating its neck. Both sexes build nest in tree or shrub, generally not far from the ground. A sharp *skeow* may be heard in flight.

Habitat

Found in a variety of wetland habitats but prefers streams, ponds, and marshes with woodland cover.

Local Sites

The Green Heron is a common breeder in wetlands statewide. Coastal marshes are a good place to find it. Listen for its distinctive call on October nights as it migrates south.

FIELD NOTES An innovative hunter, the Green Heron will sometimes, though rarely, stand at the edge of shallow water and toss twigs, insects, even earthworms into the water as lures to attract unsuspecting minnows into its striking range. This is one of the few instances of tool use in the bird world.

Breeding | Adult

Nycticorax nycticorax L 25" (64 cm) WS 44" (112 cm)

FIELD MARKS
Black crown and back

Two to three white hindneck
plumes, longest when breeding

White underparts and face; gray
wings, tail, and sides of neck

Immature streaked brown

Behavior
Primarily a nocturnal feeder. Even when feeding during
the day, remains in the shadows, almost motionless,
waiting for prey to come within range. Forages for fish,
frogs, rodents, reptiles, mollusks, eggs, and nestlings.
Black-crowneds, consumers of fairly large prey, are
susceptible to accumulating contaminants; their
population status is an indicator of environmental
quality. Call heard in flight is a gutteral *quok*.

Habitat
Has adapted to a wide range of habitats, including
salt marshes, brackish and freshwater wetlands, and
lakeshores that provide cover and forage. Nests in
colonies high up in trees.

Local Sites
The Black-crowned Night-Heron occurs commonly
during summer at Montezuma National Wildlife
Refuge and other wetlands statewide. Listen for its
sharp *whack* nocturnal call during autumn migration.

FIELD NOTES Many formerly large breeding colonies of the Black-
crowned Night-Heron have declined or disappeared in recent
decades because of loss of wetland habitat due to development
or to the effects of toxic chemicals, or to other disturbances
caused by human activities.

Year-round | Adult

TURKEY VULTURE

Cathartes aura L 27" (69 cm) W 69" (175 cm)

FIELD MARKS
Naked red head; ivory bill;
red legs

Brownish black feathers over
body; silver-gray flight feathers

In flight, contrasting underwings
show and long tail extends
beyond feet

Behavior
Soars high in search of carrion and refuse, watching for
other scavengers. Rocks from side to side in flight, seldom flapping its wings, which are held upward in a
shallow V, allowing it to gain lift from conditions that
would deter many other raptors. Feeds heavily when
food is available but can go days without if necessary.

Habitat
Hunts in open country, woodlands, farms, urban
dumps and landfills. Nests solitarily in hollow logs or,
less frequently, in hollow trees, crevices, caves, mine
shafts. The spread of Turkey Vultures in the Northeast
is considered a result of the increased number of white-
tailed deer and, consequently, increased roadkills.

Local Sites
Common statewide during migration and in summer;
in winter, restricted to the southern fringe and the
coast. Look for large concentrations in March and April
at hawkwatch sites such as Braddock Bay, Derby Hill.

FIELD NOTES The most widespread vulture in North America,
popularly known as a "buzzard," the Turkey Vulture's naked head
is an adaptation that keeps it from soiling its feathers while feeding, reducing the risk of picking up disease from carcasses. It
also has an unusually well-developed sense of smell, allowing it
to locate carrion concealed in forest settings.

Year-round | Adult

OSPREY

Pandion haliaetus L 22-25" (56-64 cm) WS 58-72" (147-183 cm)

FIELD MARKS

Dark brown above, white below;
white head, dark eye stripe;
females usually have darker neck
streaks

Slightly arched in flight, wings
appear bent back or "crooked"

Pale plumage fringing in juvenile

Behavior

Hunts by soaring, hovering, then diving down and
plunging feet-first into water, snatching its prey with
long, lethal talons. Feeds exclusively on fish. The
Osprey's specialized diet makes it susceptible to accumulating contaminants, such as DDT. Nests near bodies of fresh or salt water. Bulky nests are built atop dead
trees or on specialized man-made platforms. Call is a
series of clear, resonant, whistled *kyew*s.

Habitat

Forages in a variety of aquatic habitats, including lakes,
rivers, and reservoirs. Highly migratory, these birds can
be found on every continent except Antarctica.

Local Sites

Common on the coast from April through October, the
Osprey is easily found near the coastal bays of Long
Island, and it is common at Montezuma National
Wildlife Refuge.

FIELD NOTES The use of DDT and other chemical pollutants
during the 1950s and 1960s decimated the Osprey population in
New York. Since then, reintroduction programs and the ban of
DDT have made them once again regular breeders at lakes and
coastal areas.

Year-round | Adult

BALD EAGLE

Haliaeetus leucocephalus L 31-37" (79-94 cm) WS 70-90" (178-229 cm)

FIELD MARKS
Distinctive white head and tail

Large yellow beak, feet, and eyes

Brown body

Juveniles mostly dark, showing
blotchy white on underwing
and tail

Behavior
The national bird of the United States. A rock-steady
flier, the Bald Eagle rarely swerves or tips on its flattened wings. Feeds mainly on fish, but sometimes on
waterfowl, carrion, or small mammals. Often steals fish
from other birds of prey. Bald Eagles lock talons and
cartwheel together through the sky in an elaborate
courtship dance. Nests solitarily in tall trees or on cliffs.
Call is a weak, almost inaudible *kak-kak-kak*.

Habitat
This member of the sea-eagle group generally lives and
feeds along seacoasts or along rivers and lakes.

Local Sites
The magnificent Bald Eagle has recently rebounded in
the state and now nests at many locations. Its numbers
were reduced in the 1970s because of eggshell thinning
caused by DDT. Best bets are Montezuma National
Wildlife Refuge, along the lower Hudson River in
winter, and at Derby Hill and Braddock Bay during
spring migration.

FIELD NOTES An immature Bald Eagle (inset:
second year) shows a variable amount of white
spotting on its head, breast, and underwings.
It is not until its fifth year that it acquires the
characteristic stark white head of the adult.

Juvenile

COOPER'S HAWK

Accipiter cooperii L 14-20" (36-51 cm) WS 29-37" (74-94 cm)

FIELD MARKS

Blue-gray upperparts; reddish bars across breast, belly

Dark gray cap; bright red eyes

Long, rounded, barred tail with white terminal band

Juvenile brown with yellow eyes

Behavior
Scans for prey from a perch or while soaring; attacks with a sudden burst of speed. Flies fast and close to the ground, using brush to conceal its rapid attack. Feeds on birds, rabbits, rodents, reptiles, and insects. Known to hold prey underwater to drown it. Gives a high *kew-kew-kew* call at nest site.

Habitat
Prefers broken, especially deciduous, woodlands and streamside groves. Has adapted to fragmented woodlands created by urban and suburban development.

Local Sites
Increasing in abundance and breeding distribution in New York. Preys on birds at feeders in winter and nesting in suburban yards in summer. During spring migration large numbers are found at Derby Hill and Braddock Bay, especially in late March and April.

FIELD NOTES Distinguishing a Cooper's from a Sharp-shinned Hawk, *Accipiter striatus* (inset: juvenile, left; adult, right), is one of birding's more difficult identifications. Both species are largely brown as juveniles; blue-gray above, barred rufous below as adults. The Sharp-shinned is slightly smaller, has a squared-off tail, and its neck does not extend as far out in flight.

Year-round | Adult light morph

BROAD-WINGED HAWK

Buteo platypterus L 16" (41 cm) WS 34" (86 cm)

FIELD MARKS

Dark brown above; adult pale
below with rufous barring;
immature darkly streaked below

In flight, white underwings have
dark borders

Short, broad tail has black and
white bands

Behavior

In fall, migrates in large flocks, called kettles, often
composed of thousands of birds. Perches near water at
the edge of woods, then swoops down on its prey of
amphibians, reptiles, rodents, small birds, and large
insects. Nests of the Broad-winged, composed of sticks,
leaves, bark, and lichen, are built in trees by both the
male and female in a process which can last up to five
weeks. Its call is a thin, shrill, slightly descending whistle of *kee-eee*, easily imitated by Blue Jays.

Habitat

Breeds in deciduous forests of the eastern woodlands of
North America. Winters primarily in the Amazon River
region of South America.

Local Sites

The Broad-winged Hawk breeds throughout the state,
but it is easiest to see during spring migration at Braddock Bay and Derby Hill, where thousands pass in
late April.

FIELD NOTES The related Red-shouldered Hawk,
Buteo lineatus (inset), is a slightly larger bird. It has
spotted brown plumage with reddish shoulders,
wing linings, and chest; and a long tail
with narrow white tail bands.

Year-round | Adult

RED-TAILED HAWK

Buteo jamaicensis L 22" (56 cm) WS 50" (127 cm)

FIELD MARKS

Brown above; red tail on adults

Whitish belly with broad band of
dark streaking

Dark bar on leading edge
of underwing

Immature has brown, banded tail

Behavior

Watch for the Red-tailed Hawk circling above, searching for rodents, sometimes kiting, or hanging motionless on the wind. Uses thermals to gain lift, conserving
its energy while soaring. Perches for long intervals on
telephone poles and other man-made structures, often
in urban areas. Nests in large trees, on cliffs, or on
man-made structures; often uses old nests abandoned
by other hawks. Listen for its distinctive call, a harsh,
rising then descending *shee-eeee-arrr.*

Habitat

Found in a variety of habitats from woods to prairies
to farmland, and even in urban settings. Common at
habitat edges, where field meets forest or wetlands meet
woodlands, favored for the variety of prey found there.

Local Sites

New York's most common resident hawk is
conspicuous at all seasons when perched along roadsides and circling above highways throughout the state.

FIELD NOTES While perched, Red-taileds are easy to spot, but
when migrating, the hawks soar at altitudes up to 5,000 feet,
appearing as nothing more than specks in the sky.

Year-round | Adult male

AMERICAN KESTREL

Falco sparverius L 10.5" (27 cm) WS 23" (58 cm)

FIELD MARKS

Russet back and tail; streaked
tawny to pale underparts

Two black stripes on white face

Male has blue-gray wing coverts

Female has russet wing coverts
and russet streaks on her breast

Behavior

Feeds on insects, reptiles, mice and other small
mammals. Hovers over prey, then plunges down for the
kill. Will also feed on small birds, especially in winter.
Regularly seen perched on fences and telephone lines,
bobbing its tail with frequency. Nests in tree holes,
barns, or man-made boxes using little or no nesting
material. Has clear, shrill call of *killy-killy-killy* or
klee-klee-klee, given year-round.

Habitat

North America's most widely distributed falcon, found
in open country and in cities, often mousing along
highway medians or sweeping along riparian areas.

Local Sites

The American Kestrel is a year-round resident, but it is
easiest to find during spring migration at Derby Hill
and Braddock Bay and during fall migration anywhere
on the coast, especially at the Fire Island hawkwatch.

FIELD NOTES The American Kestrel is sometimes called a "Sparrow Hawk," but this is a misnomer because the species does not
consume a significant number of sparrows. It feeds mainly on
insects and small vertebrates such as reptiles, frogs, and, occasionally, small bats.

Immature

PEREGRINE FALCON

Falco peregrinus L 16-20" (41-51 cm) WS 36-44" (91-112 cm)

FIELD MARKS

Blue-black crown and nape

Black extends below eye, forming distinctive "helmet"

Adult shows rufous wash below

Juvenile is brownish above; underparts heavily streaked

Behavior

An incredibly fast raptor; hunts by flying high on powerful wingbeats, then swooping in on prey in a spectactular dive that can clock in at 175 mph or more. Also flies low over water to surprise waterfowl prey. Feeds primarily on birds, the larger of which may be knocked out of the air and subsequently eaten on the ground. Nests on cliffs, bridges, or tall buildings with very little nesting material. Though usually silent, gives out loud *kak-kak-kak* call at nesting area.

Habitat

Traditionally breeds near cliffs; but now also established in cities. Hunts a wide area and in a variety of habitats.

Local Sites

The Peregrine Falcon nests in several locations in the state, including New York City, and is easily observed as a migrant in early October at the Fire Island hawkwatch.

FIELD NOTES The Merlin, *Falco columbarius* (inset: male, left; female, right), is another fast, powerful, and aggressive falcon that visits New York primarily on migration. It is smaller than the Peregrine and lacks the Peregrine's distinctive "helmeted" look.

Year-round | Adult

AMERICAN COOT

Fulica americana L 15.5" (39 cm)

FIELD MARKS
Blackish head; slate gray body

Small, reddish brown forehead
shield; reddish eyes on adult

Whitish bill with dark band at tip;
greenish legs with lobed toes

Juvenile paler with darker bill

Behavior
The coot's distinctive toes are flexible and lobed, permitting it to swim well and to dive for aquatic vegetation and invertebrates. Runs on water, flapping wings rapidly to gain momentum to take flight. Bobs its small head back and forth when walking or swimming. Forages in large flocks, especially during winter. Makes a floating nest anchored to aquatic vegetation. Has a wide vocabulary of grunts, cackles, and chatter.

Habitat
Breeds in freshwater marshes or on lakes and ponds. Winters on both fresh and salt water. The coot has also adapted to human-altered habitats, including sewage lagoons for foraging.

Local Sites
The American Coot is common year-round at most wetlands. Large concentrations occur during migration and winter, especially on the Finger Lakes.

FIELD NOTES The Common Moorhen, *Gallinula chloropus* (inset), inhabits many of the same freshwater wetlands as the coot. It has a bright red forehead shield which extends onto a red bill tipped with yellow.

Year-round | Adult

KILLDEER

Charadrius vociferus L 10.5" (27 cm)

FIELD MARKS

Gray-brown above; white neck
and belly; two black breast bands

Black stripe on forehead and one
extending back from black bill

Red-orange rump visible in flight

Red orbital ring

Behavior

Often seen running, then stopping on a dime with an
inquisitive look, then suddenly jabbing at the ground
with its bill. Feeds mainly on insects that live in short
vegetation. May gather in loose flocks, but more often
seen by itself. Builds its nest on almost any open
ground, even in residential areas. Listen for its loud,
piercing, eponymous call of *kill-dee* or its rising *dee-
dee-dee*. Also gives a long, trilled *trrrrrrr* during
courtship display or when its nest is threatened.

Habitat

Although a type of plover—one of the shorebirds—the
Killdeer prefers inland grassy regions, but may also be
found on shores.

Local Sites

Noisy and active, the abundant Killdeer is easy to find
in fields, pastures, golf courses, urban parks, and at the
edges of lakes and ponds.

FIELD NOTES The Semipalmated Plover,
Charadrius semipalmatus (inset), an abundant
migrant found on mudflats, is smaller than the
Killdeer, has one breast band, a stubby
orange-and-black bill, yellow-orange legs.

Nonbreeding | Adult

GREATER YELLOWLEGS

Tringa melanoleuca L 14" (36 cm)

FIELD MARKS

Long, dark, slightly upturned bill; long, bright yellow-orange legs

Head and neck streaked gray-brown; white-speckled, gray-brown back

White underparts slightly barred gray-brown on flanks

Behavior

A predator of snails, crabs, and shrimp; also skims surface of water for insects and larvae. Sprints short distances in pursuit of small fish. Usually seen alone or in small groups, this wary bird sounds an alarm when a hawk or falcon approaches. Call is distinctive series of three or more loud, repeated, descending *tew-tew-tew* sounds, heard most often in flight.

Habitat

In winter, frequents a full range of wetlands, including marshes, ponds, lakes, rivers, and reservoirs. Breeds across the Canadian boreal zone.

Local Sites

Most conspicuous during fall migration, the Greater Yellowlegs passes through on its way from the Arctic. Look for it in coastal marshes, especially at Jamaica Bay, and inland at Montezuma National Wildlife Refuge.

FIELD NOTES The Lesser Yellowlegs, *Tringa flavipes* (inset), shares much of the Greater's habitat. Distinguished by its shorter, straighter bill—about the length of its head—it is smaller in stature and less wary in behavior. The Lesser's call is higher and shorter too, consisting of one or two *tew* notes.

Breeding | Adult

SPOTTED SANDPIPER

Actitis macularius L 7.5" (19 cm)

FIELD MARKS

Olive-brown upperparts, barred
during breeding season

White underparts, spotted brown
while breeding

Short, straight orange bill tipped
in black; short white wing stripe
in flight

Behavior

Often seen singly, feeding on insects, crustaceans, and
other invertebrates by plucking them from the water's
surface or snatching them from the air. Walks with a
constant teetering motion. Flies with stiff, shallow
wingbeats. The slightly larger female is the first to
establish territory and to defend it during breeding season. Nests on grass near water. Calls include a shrill
peet-weet and a series of *weet* notes, given in flight.

Habitat

Inhabits sheltered ponds, lakes, streams, and marshes.

Local Sites

The Spotted Sandpiper is a common breeder at wetlands in most of the state. Listen for its distinctive *swee-
swee* call during nocturnal migration in September.

FIELD NOTES A regular migrant across the state, the Solitary
Sandpiper, *Tringa solitaria* (inset: breed-
ing), has a longer neck than the Spotted;
its lower throat, breast, and sides are
streaked blackish brown; its brown upperparts are heavily spotted buffy white; and
it has a bold white eye ring. Its call is
higher pitched and more emphatic.

Nonbreeding | Adult

LEAST SANDPIPER

Calidris minutilla L 6" (15 cm)

FIELD MARKS
Short, thin, slightly decurved bill
Gray-brown upperparts
Streaked gray-brown breast band
White belly and undertail coverts
Yellowish to greenish legs

Behavior
Forages for food with its short, spiky bill. Feeds on worms, insects, mollusks, small crabs, and fish in muddy, sandy, or shallow water. Not wary of humans, it will investigate picnic sites on beaches. If flushed, flies off rapidly in a zigzag flight pattern. The Least Sandpiper's call is a high *kree* or *jeet*.

Habitat
Found in tidal coastal regions and wetlands with exposed mud or sand. Breeds in the Arctic.

Local Sites
A widespread migrant during spring and fall, the Least Sandpiper often prefers to stay farther from the water than other shorebirds. Look for it on mudflats statewide during May and August.

FIELD NOTES The Semipalmated Sandpiper, *Calidris pusilla* (inset, from left: breeding; juvenile; winter), migrates through New York in spring and fall. It looks and behaves much like the Least Sandpiper, but is distinguished by black legs, slightly larger size, and a heavier bill.

Breeding | Adult

WILLET

Catoptrophorus semipalmatus L 15" (38 cm)

FIELD MARKS

Large, plump, with long gray legs

Breeding adult is heavily mottled; white belly

Winter plumage pale gray above

In flight, shows black-and-white wing pattern with black edges

Behavior

The Willet, like other shorebirds, wades in search of prey, probing through mud with its long bill. Feeds primarily on aquatic insects and their larvae. While generally protective as parents, Willets are known to leave unhatched eggs behind once the first young leave the nest. Its breeding call of *pill-will-willet* is the origin of its name; it may also be heard giving a *kip-kip-kip* alarm call.

Habitat

Nests in a variety of coastal wetlands during spring and summer months, sometimes within 200 feet of another Willet nest. Moves south in winter.

Local Sites

As a breeder, the Willet is restricted to coastal marshes in New York. Look for it in the back bays of Long Island and at Jamaica Bay and watch for the larger and paler *inornatus* subspecies arriving from the West in late summer and fall.

FIELD NOTES A common migrant, the Pectoral Sandpiper, *Calidris melanotos* (inset, juvenile) has upperparts richly patterned in black, rusty, and white. It is most easily identified by the sharp boundary between its darkly streaked breast and pure white belly.

Year-round | Adult

AMERICAN WOODCOCK

Scolopax minor L 11" (28 cm)

FIELD MARKS

Chunky; mottled brown and gray above and orange-brown below

Long, stout bill

Short neck, legs, and tail

Large eyes set high in the head

Rounded wings

Behavior

This secretive bird is most often spotted at dusk. It uses its long bill to probe deep into the damp earth of the forest floor for its favorite meal of earthworms. Also eats millipedes, beetles, and flies. Its flexible upper bill tip allows it to snatch prey below ground. If flushed, it will fly up abruptly, its wings making a loud, twittering sound. Its nasal *peent* is heard mainly in spring.

Habitat

Although a shorebird, the American Woodcock prefers moist woodlands, where it nests on the forest floor.

Local Sites

The amazing aerial displays of the American Woodcock can be heard over fallow farm fields from April onward. At dusk listen for the spinning-rusty-wheel sounds of the male's courtship display.

FIELD NOTES The slightly smaller Wilson's Snipe, *Gallinago delicata* (inset), has a long bill for probing the mud of wetlands. It has a boldly striped head and barred flanks. In swooping display flights, its vibrating outer tail feathers make quavering hoots.

Breeding | Adult

BONAPARTE'S GULL

Larus philadelphia L 13.5" (34 cm) WS 33" (84 cm)

FIELD MARKS

Breeding adult has black hood, absent in winter adult

Gray mantle and upperwings

Black-and-white wingtips, pale on underside; white underparts

Black bill; orange-red legs

Behavior

Among the smallest and most graceful of North American gulls. Though it is omnivorous and willing to forage on a variety of prey, it seldom feeds at garbage dumps, unlike most other gulls. Often forages in large flocks, and will gather at river mouths, diving for small fish and wading for fish eggs. Gives low, raspy chatters and single *mew* calls.

Habitat

Favors marine environments during winter, but stops off at lakes, ponds, rivers, and marshes on migration. Breeds in coniferous forests of Canada and Alaska.

Local Sites

The Bonaparte's Gull is abundant on the Niagara River during migration in late November, and large numbers sometimes remain there through the winter.

FIELD NOTES Most birds on spring migration show the full black hood of the breeding adult (opposite), but on fall migration, look for the less distinct dark spots behind the eyes of the winter adult (inset). Immature Bonaparte's Gulls show some brown on wings and a dark tail band.

Nonbreeding | Adult

RING-BILLED GULL

Larus delawarensis L 17.5" (44 cm) WS 48" (122 cm)

FIELD MARKS
Adult: Yellow bill with black subterminal ring; pale eye with dark
orbital ring

Pale gray upperparts; white
underparts; yellowish legs; black
primaries show white spots

Head streaked light brown in winter

Behavior
This opportunistic feeder will scavenge for garbage,
grains, dead fish, fruit, and marine invertebrates. A
vocal gull, it calls, croaks, and cries incessantly,
especially during feeding. The call consists of a series
of laughing croaks that begins with a short, gruff note
and falls into a series of *kheeyaahhh* sounds.

Habitat
Common along shorelines in winter, but also a regular
visitor to most inland bodies of water, especially
reservoirs in urban areas.

Local Sites
A common migrant and winter resident throughout
the state, the Ring-billed Gull breeds on small islands
in the Great Lakes and at various locations upstate.
Visit your nearest fast-food parking lot, and you should
find this species feeding on French fries.

FIELD NOTES The Ring-billed along with its
partner in crime, the Herring Gull, *Larus
argentatus* (inset: nonbreeding), are the two
quintessential "seagulls." Adults are similar in
plumage color and pattern, but the Herring
Gull is noticeably larger with a red spot on
its lower mandible and pinkish legs.

Year-round | Adult

GREAT BLACK-BACKED GULL

Larus marinus L 30" (76 cm) WS 65" (165 cm)

FIELD MARKS

Large gull; adult has large yellow bill with red spot on lower mandible

Black mantle and upper wing; white head, neck, and underparts

White primary tips, tail, and uppertail coverts; pink legs

Behavior

The largest gull in the world, the Great Black-backed will bully smaller gulls and take their lunches. Also scavenges on beaches for mollusks, crustaceans, insects, and eggs; wades in water for fish, roots through garbage for carrion and refuse, and even kills birds as large as cormorants. On breeding grounds, listen for a low, slow *keeeeyaaaahh*.

Habitat

Coastal areas of eastern North America and large inland lakes and rivers. Breeding range is extending southward along the Atlantic coast.

Local Sites

The Great Black-backed Gull is a year-round resident on large bodies of water including the coast, the Finger Lakes, and Lake Ontario. The best place to see it is along the coast of Long Island.

FIELD NOTES The Lesser Black-backed Gull, *Larus fuscus* (inset: nonbreeding), is actually dark gray on its back and wings and resembles the Herring Gull (preceding page), but is darker above and has yellow legs. With numbers steadily increasing, the Lesser Black-backeds can now be found regularly in winter on the Niagara River and the coast.

Breeding | Adult

CASPIAN TERN

Sterna caspia L 21" (53 cm) WS 50" (127 cm)

FIELD MARKS

Large, thick, red bill with dark tip

Pale gray above, white below

Breeding adult has black cap;
winter adult's crown is dusky

In flight, shows dark primary tips
and slightly forked tail

Behavior

Usually solitary, often hovers before diving for small
fish, its main food. Also swims gull-like and feeds from
the water's surface. Largest of the terns, the Caspian
frequently steals catches from other gulls and terns, and
feeds on their eggs and chicks. Adult calls include a loud
rasping *rraah* or *ahhrr* and a drawn-out, upslurred
rrah-ah-ahr. Juvenile call when begging for food is a
high, thin whistled *ssiiuuh*.

Habitat

Locally common and widespread on coastlines world-
wide. Small colonies nest together on beaches or on
islands of inland rivers.

Local Sites

The Caspian Tern breeds in only two places in New
York, but it occurs regularly as a migrant during spring
and fall. It is easy to see at Montezuma National
Wildlife Refuge in August, at Derby Hill in April, and
along the coast during fall migration.

FIELD NOTES The Caspian Tern, named for the Caspian Sea in
southern Russia, is among the world's most widely distributed
terns, nesting on five continents. It is absent as a breeder only
from Antarctica and South America.

Breeding | Adult

COMMON TERN

Sterna hirundo L 11.5-12.5" (29-32 cm) WS 29.5-32.5" (75-83 cm)

FIELD MARKS

Long wings; long forked tail

Breeding adult: mostly red bill;
complete black cap; pale gray
upperwings; red legs

Winter adult, immature: white
forehead; black bill and legs

Behavior

Sleek, fast, and graceful, the Common Tern feeds on
small fish by flying over water, hovering when it spots
prey, then diving to catch the fish at or below the surface. Breeds in large colonies, sometimes numbering
in the thousands, on barrier beaches, islands, dredge
spoils, and lake shores. Nest is a shallow scrape on
bare sand or soil, usually lined with dead plant material and other shoreline debris. Most distinctive in a
varied repertoire of calls is a long, piercing *kee-arr.*

Habitat

Common, locally abundant breeder and migrant on
sea coasts, inland lakes, major rivers. Winters along
coasts of Central and South America, rarely on the
U. S. Gulf Coast.

Local Sites

The Common Tern breeds abundantly on Long
Island; occurs widely but scarcely as a breeder and
migrant. Look for it in summer and early fall along
the Long Island coast, where it fishes in the surf.

FIELD NOTES The Forster's Tern, *Sterna
forsteri* (inset, breeding adult), differs from the
Common Tern by a more robust body, bright
white outerwings and underparts, a thicker and
mostly orange bill, and a more labored, moth-
like flight.

Year-round | Adult

ROCK PIGEON

Columba livia L 12.5" (32 cm)

FIELD MARKS

Variably plumaged, with head and
neck usually darker than back

White cere at base of dark bill,
pink legs

Iridescent feathers on neck reflect
green, bronze, and purple

Behavior

Feeds on grain, seeds, fruit, and refuse; a frequent
visitor to farms and backyard feeding stations. As it
forages, moves with a short-stepped, "pigeon-toed" gait
while its head bobs back and forth. Courtship display
consists of male puffing out neck feathers, fanning tail,
and turning in circles while cooing. Nests and roosts
primarily on high window ledges, on bridges, and in
barns. Characterized by soft *coo-cuk-cuk-cuk-cooo* call.

Habitat

Introduced from Europe in the 1600s, the Rock Pigeon
is now found almost anywhere near human habitation.

Local Sites

The familiar beggar and street-cleaner is common in
almost every city and town, and large flocks live in
many farmyards.

FIELD NOTES The Rock Pigeon's variable colors, ranging
from rust red to all white to mosaic (inset), were
developed over centuries of near domestica-
tion. The pigeons that most resemble their
wild ancestors have a dark head and
neck, two black wing bars, a white
rump, and a black terminal band
on the tail.

Year-round | Adult

MOURNING DOVE

Zenaida macroura L 12" (31 cm)

FIELD MARKS

Gray-brown; black spots on upper wings; white tips on outer tail feathers show in flight

Trim-bodied; long pointed tail

Black spot on lower cheek; pinkish wash on neck.

Behavior
Generally a ground feeder, the Mourning Dove forages for grains, seeds, grasses, and insects. Like other *Columbidae*, it is able to slurp up water without tipping back its head. The Mourning Dove is aggressively territorial while nesting, but will gather into large roosting flocks after breeding season. Also known to produce multiple broods a season. Wings produce a fluttering whistle as the bird takes flight. Known for its mournful call, *oowooo-woo-woo-woo*, given by males during breeding season.

Habitat
Widespread and abundant, the Mourning Dove is found in a variety of habitats, but prefers open areas, often choosing suburban sites for feeding and nesting.

Local Sites
Abundant throughout the state, these birds can be found in virtually every habitat except deep forests.

FIELD NOTES The Mourning Dove, like other members of the family *Columbidae*, has the ability to produce "pigeon milk" in its crop lining. It regurgitates this substance to its young during their first few days. In appearance and nutritious content, it is remarkably similar to the milk of mammals.

Year-round | Adult

YELLOW-BILLED CUCKOO

Coccyzus americanus L 12" (31 cm)

FIELD MARKS

Gray-brown above, mostly white below; yellow orbital ring

Decurved bill with dark upper mandible and yellow lower

Underside of tail patterned in bold black and white

Behavior

This shy species slips quietly through woodlands, combing vegetation for caterpillars and insects. During courtship, male climbs on female's shoulders to feed her from above. Builds nest of grasses and moss on horizontal tree limb. Unique song sounds hollow and wooden, a rapid staccato *kuk-kuk-kuk*, usually descending to a *kakakowlp-kowlp* ending; it is often heard just before a storm in spring and summer.

Habitat

Common in dense canopies of woods, orchards, and streamside groves. Also inhabits tangles of swamp edges. Winters in South America.

Local Sites

The Yellow-billed Cuckoo is more often heard than seen, making its presence known by its characteristic guttural vocalizations. Look for it during summer in deciduous woodlands statewide, and in varied habitats during fall migration.

FIELD NOTES The closely related Black-billed Cuckoo, *Coccyzus erythropthalmus* (inset), is known to sometimes lay its eggs in the nests of Yellow-billeds. It is best distinguished by its dark bill and red eye ring.

Year-round | Adult

BARN OWL

Tyto alba L 16" (41 cm) WS 42" (107 cm)

FIELD MARKS

White heart-shaped face

Dark eyes, pale bill

Rusty brown above; cinnamon-barred wings

White to pale cinnamon spotted underparts, darker on females

Behavior

A nocturnal predator on rodents, small birds, bats, snakes, and insects. Hunts in pastures and marshes. Wing feathers with loosely knit edges and soft body plumage make its flight almost soundless—effective in surprising prey. Roosts and nests at all times of year in dark cavities in city and farm buildings, in burrows, cliff holes, and hollow trees. Song is a long, raspy, hissing shriek, often repeated.

Habitat

Distributed throughout the world, the Barn Owl is found in urban, suburban, rural, and other open regions throughout its range.

Local Sites

The severely declining Barn Owl is becoming hard to find in most of the state, but can be seen fairly commonly where special nest boxes have been installed in tidal marshes on Long Island.

FIELD NOTES The Barn Owl hunts primarily by sound. With its asymmetrically placed ear openings, it can pinpoint the location of its prey even in total darkness

Year-round | Adult rufous morph

EASTERN SCREECH-OWL

Megascops asio L 8.5" (22 cm)

FIELD MARKS

Small; with yellow eyes and pale tip on yellow-green bill

Rufous and gray morphs occur

Underparts marked by vertical streaks crossed by dark bars

Ear tufts prominent if raised

Behavior

Nocturnal; uses exceptional vision and hearing to hunt for mice, voles, shrews, and insects. Seeks out densest and thickest cover available for daytime roost and, if approached, will stretch its body, erect its ear tufts, and shut its eyes to blend into background. Nests in tree cavities about 10 to 30 feet up. Emits a series of quavering trills, descending in pitch, when defending territory; and a long, low-pitched trill around the nest site.

Habitat

Found in a wide variety of habitats including woodlots, forests, swamps, parks, and suburban gardens.

Local Sites

The Eastern Screech-Owl's "whinny" and "trilling" vocalizations are regular features of late-spring and early-fall nights in mixed woodlands and parks. Look for them by day in tree cavities, where their plumage, looking like bark, makes them difficult to see.

FIELD NOTES New York's smallest owl, only about the size of a robin, the Northern Saw-whet, *Aegolius acadicus* (inset), is difficult to study due to its elusive nature and diminutive size. Saw-whets may be more common than peviously thought, and banding programs indicate that fairly large numbers migrate through the state.

Year-round | Adult

GREAT HORNED OWL

Bubo virginianus L 22" (56 cm) WS 54" (137 cm)

FIELD MARKS

Mottled brownish gray above, densely barred below

Long ear tufts, or "horns"

Rust-colored facial disks

Yellow eyes; white chin and throat; buff-colored underwings

Behavior
Chiefly nocturnal. Watches from perch, then swoops down on prey, which includes cats, skunks, porcupines, birds, snakes, rodents, and frogs. Reuses abandoned nests of other large birds. Begins nesting by February, possibly to take advantage of winter-stressed prey. Territorial song, often sung in duet, consists of three to eight loud, deep hoots, the second and third often short and rapid. Song mostly heard at dusk and dawn.

Habitat
The most widespread owl in North America, the Great Horned Owl can be found in a wide variety of habitats including forests, cities, and farmlands.

Local Sites
One of the year's earliest breeding birds, the Great Horned Owl is nesting by January in many locations. Look for its nest in deciduous trees before leaf-out, when the female's ear tufts are visible above the nest's twigs.

FIELD NOTES Only slightly smaller than the Great Horned, the Barred Owl, *Strix varia* (inset), also inhabits a variety of woodlands in New York. Its loud rhythmic call, *who-cooks-for-you*, *who-cooks-for-you-all*, is much more likely to be heard during the day than most owls' calls.

Year-round | Adult

COMMON NIGHTHAWK

Chordeiles minor L 9.5" (24 cm)

FIELD MARKS

Dark gray-brown mottled back;
bold white bar across primaries

Long, pointed wings with pale
spotting; tail slightly forked

Underparts whitish with bold
dusky bars; bar on tail in males

Behavior
Hunts in flight, snaring insects; streamlined body
allows agile aerial maneuvers. Drops lower jaw to
create opening wide enough to take in even large
moths. Skims over surface of lakes to drink. Roosts on
the ground and on branches, posts, or roofs. Nests on
the ground or on gravel rooftops. Male's wings make
hollow booming sound during diving courtship
display. Male gives a nasal *peent* in flight.

Habitat
Frequents woodlands, shrubby areas, and urban and
suburban settings. Winters in South America.

Local Sites
A declining species, the Common Nighthawk is best
sought on the coast during fall migration in late August
and September. It can be seen by day at this time, often
during the afternoon.

FIELD NOTES Another nighttime insect hunter of summer, the
Whip-poor-will, *Caprimulgus vociferus* (inset),
hunts in flight for moths and mosquitoes
and roosts on the ground during the day. It
is most easily identified in the field by its
loud, melodious song: *WHIP poor WILL.*

Year-round | Adult

CHIMNEY SWIFT

Chaetura pelagica L 5.3" (13 cm)

FIELD MARKS
Short, cigar-shaped body

Long, pointed, narrow wings

Dark plumage, sooty gray overall

Short, stubby tail

Blackish gray bill, legs, feet

Behavior
Crisscrosses the sky with rapid wingbeats of long wings at high speeds, snatching up ants, termites, and spiders while in flight. Look for groups of migrating Chimney Swifts circling above rooftops at dusk before dropping into chimneys or steeples to roost. Builds cup-shaped nest of twigs glued together with dried saliva in chimneys, barn eaves, hollow trees. During aerial courtship, the male raises his wings into a sharp V. Call, given in-flight, is a rapid, continual, high-pitched chattering.

Habitat
Often seen soaring over forested, open, suburban, and urban areas. Winters as far south as Peru.

Local Sites
Common breeders in many urban areas, where they also gather in large "staging" roosts in chimneys before and during migration. In spring migration at Braddock Bay and Derby Hill, as well as at local roost sites, thousands may be seen to disappear into a single chimney.

FIELD NOTES The Chimney Swift once confined its nests to tree hollows and other natural sites. Over the centuries, it has adapted so well to artificial nesting sites such as chimneys, air shafts, vertical pipes, barns, and silos, that the species' numbers have increased dramatically. It is the only swift seen regularly in the eastern United States.

Year-round | Adult male

RUBY-THROATED HUMMINGBIRD

Archilochus colubris L 3.8" (10 cm)

FIELD MARKS
Metallic green above

Adult male has brilliant red gorget, black chin, whitish underparts, dusky green sides

Female lacks gorget, has whitish throat and underparts, and a buffy wash on sides

Behavior
Probes backyard hummingbird feeders and flowers for nectar by hovering virtually still in midair. Also feeds on small spiders and insects. When nectar is scarce, known to drink sap from wells made in tree trunks by sapsuckers. In spring, male Ruby-throateds arrive in breeding territory before females and engage in jousts to claim prime territory. Once mated, females build nests on small tree limbs and raise young by themselves. In addition to the "hum" generated by its rapidly beating wings, this bird emits soft *tchew* notes.

Habitat
Found in gardens and woodland edges throughout most of the eastern United States.

Local Sites
New York's only nesting hummingbird, the Ruby-throated Hummingbird is widespread as a breeder and migrant. It commonly visits feeders in summer and zips along the coast during migration in September.

FIELD NOTES Hummingbirds and the flowers they pollinate have evolved to meet each other's needs. Typical flowers favored by the birds are narrow and tubular, the nectar accessible only to a long bill or tongue. The hummingbird is attracted to the flowers' bright colors; a sign, perhaps, of the nectar within.

Immature

BELTED KINGFISHER

Ceryle alcyon L 13" (33 cm)

FIELD MARKS
Blue-gray head with large,
shaggy crest

Blue-gray upperparts and breast
band; white underparts and collar

Long, heavy, black bill

Female: Chestnut sides and belly band

Behavior
Generally solitary and vocal, dives headfirst for fish from
a waterside perch or after hovering above in order to line
up on its target. Also feeds on insects, amphibians, and
small reptiles. Monogamous pairs nest in burrows they
dig together three or more feet into vertical earthen
banks near watery habitats. Both male and female share
in parenting duties as well. Mated pairs renew their
relationship each breeding season with courtship ritu-
als such as dramatic display flights, the male's feeding
of the female, and vocalizations. Call is a loud, dry rat-
tle; it is given when alarmed, to announce territory, or
while in flight. Also makes harsh *caar* notes.

Habitat
Conspicuous along rivers, ponds, lakes, and coastal
estuaries. Prefers partially wooded areas.

Local Sites
The Belted Kingfisher is a conspicuous breeder at
waterways statewide. Its only requirements seem to be
open water and an ample supply of small fish. Look for
it along the coast during winter.

FIELD NOTES The Belted Kingfisher female is one of the few in
North America that is more colorful than her male counterpart,
which lacks the female's chestnut band across the belly and
chestnut sides and flanks.

Year-round | Adult male

RED-BELLIED WOODPECKER

Melanerpes carolinus L 9.3" (24 cm)

FIELD MARKS

Black-and-white barred back

Red nape, extending onto crown only on males

Mostly grayish underparts; small reddish tinge on belly

Central tail feathers barred

Behavior

Climbs tree trunks by bracing itself with stiff tail, taking strain off short legs. Uses chisel-shaped bill to drill cavities in tree bark for nest holes and to extract grubs and insects. Also feeds on worms, fruits, seeds, and sap. Will visit backyard feeders for sunflower seeds and peanut butter. Nests and roosts at night in tree cavities. Call during breeding season is a rolling *churrr*. Also gives a conversational *chiv chiv* all year.

Habitat

Common in open woodlands, forest edges, suburbs, and parks.

Local Sites

Increasing statewide in abundance and range, the Red-bellied Woodpecker is conspicuous in all of its varied habitats.

FIELD NOTES The Red-headed Woodpecker, *Melanerpes erythrocephalus* (inset: adult, left; juvenile, right), shares much of the Red-bellied's range, but is much less common. The adult Red-headed is identified by its bright red hood and its stark white rump and underparts. The juvenile has a brownish hood and back.

Year-round | Adult male

YELLOW-BELLIED SAPSUCKER

Sphyrapicus varius L 8.5" (22 cm)

FIELD MARKS

Red forecrown on black-and-white head; chin, throat red on male, white on female

Back blackish with white barring; white rump and wing patch

Pale yellow wash on underparts

Behavior
Alone or in a pair, drills rows of evenly spaced holes in trees, then feeds on sap produced and insects attracted. Guards these wells fiercely from other birds and mammals. Also eats fruits, berries, and tree buds. Courtship ritual includes incessantly loud drumming by both male and female, *hoy-hoy* cries, and dual tapping at nest entrance. Though often silent, the Yellow-bellied sometimes makes a low, plaintive *meeww* call, or a territorial call of *quee-ark*.

Habitat
The most highly migratory of all North American woodpeckers, found in deciduous and mixed forests.

Local Sites
The Yellow-bellied Sapsucker breeds most commonly at relatively high elevations. Look for its characteristic "drillings" that appear as rows of holes in bark. A good place to find it is at Sapsucker Woods in Ithaca. During fall migration it can be conspicuous along the coast.

FIELD NOTES The bone and muscle structure of a woodpecker's head is an effective shock absorber, a necessary adaptation for a bird that spends its time drilling into hard wood. Similarly, a stiff tail and sharp claws help to maintain the bird's upright position against a tree trunk.

Year-round | Adult female

DOWNY WOODPECKER

Picoides pubescens L 6.8" (17 cm)

FIELD MARKS

Black cap, ear patch, moustachial
stripe; black wings spotted white

Blaze of white on back

White tuft in front of eyes;
whitish underparts

Red occipital patch on male

Behavior

The smallest woodpecker in North America forages
mainly on insects, larvae, and eggs. Readily visits backyard feeders for sunflower seeds and suet. Will also
consume poison ivy berries. Small size enables the
Downy to forage on very small, thin limbs. Nests in
cavities of dead trees. Both male and female stake
territorial claims with their drumming. Call is a high-
pitched but soft *pik.* Also gives a high, accelerating
whinny, *kee-kee-kee-kee.*

Habitat

Found in suburbs, parks, and orchards, as well as
forests and woodlands.

Local Sites

The Downy is easy to find in any woodlands, even in
cities. Suet feeders attract them readily in winter.

FIELD NOTES The larger and less common Hairy
Woodpecker, *Picoides villosus* (inset: male), is similarly marked but has a bill as long as its head and a
sharper, louder, lower-pitched call. It also tends to
stay on tree trunks or larger limbs than the Downy.
Note as well the all-white outer tail feathers of the
Hairy Woodpecker; the Downy's outer tail feathers
are often spotted black.

Year-round | Adult female "Yellow-shafted"

NORTHERN FLICKER

Colaptes auratus L 12.5" (32 cm)

FIELD MARKS
White rump, yellowish underwing

Brown, barred back, cream
underparts with black spotting,
and black crescent bib

Gray crown, tan face, red
crescent on nape, and, on male,
black moustachial stripe

Behavior
Feeds mostly on the ground, foraging primarily for
ants. A cavity-nesting bird, the flicker drills into almost
any wooden surface, including utility poles and
houses. An insectivore, the flicker is at least partially
migratory, traveling in the winter in pursuit of food.
Bows to its partner before engaging in courtship dance
of exaggerated wing and tail movements. Call is a
single, loud *klee-yer* heard year-round or a long series
of *wick wick wick wick* during breeding season. The
latter call is sometimes held for up to 15 seconds.

Habitat
Found in open woodlands and wooded suburban areas.

Local Sites
Attention-getters with their loud calls, these large
woodpeckers are found in any woodland. Unlike most
other woodpecker species, they can often be seen
poking into the grass for grubs and ants on lawns.

FIELD NOTES The western, or "Red-shafted," form of Northern
Flicker has pinkish underwings, a grayish face, and a red moustachial stripe on the male. These birds are accidental visitors to
the eastern United States. Hybrids may show intermediate
characteristics of both forms.

Year-round | Adult male

PILEATED WOODPECKER

Dryocopus pileatus   L 16.5" (42 cm)

FIELD MARKS

Almost entirely black on back and wings when perched

Black, white, and red striped head; red "moustache" on male

Red cap extends to bill on male

Juvenile browner overall

Behavior

Drills long, distinctively rectangular holes on tree trunks, searching for beetle larvae and other insects. Also digs into ground, stumps, and fallen logs, feeding on carpenter ants, beetles, acorns, seeds, and fruit. Nests in cavities excavated in dead or live trees, sometimes utility poles. Calls include a loud *wuk* note and a long, irregularly delivered series of *kee kee kee kee*. Also known for slow, but powerfully loud, territorial drumming, which can be heard a mile or more away.

Habitat

Prefers dense, mature forests; also found in smaller woodlots and some parks.

Local Sites

The largest of our woodpeckers, the Pileated is more often heard than seen. Listen for its loud *ke,ke,ke,ke,ke* vocalization ringing through the woods. This species is often shy, but it can be observed in deciduous woodlands throughout the state.

FIELD NOTES The excavations of the Pileated are so extensive and deep that they may fell small trees. These holes can also attract other species, such as wrens and other woodpeckers, which use the large holes for both foraging and nesting.

Breeding | Adult

LEAST FLYCATCHER

Empidonax minimus L 5.3" (13 cm)

FIELD MARKS

Bold, white eye ring; two prominent white or buffy wing bars

Grayish olive upperparts; whitish throat; pale gray underparts

Behavior

The smallest and liveliest flycatcher in eastern North America; often flicks its wings and tail upward while perched. It watches from a branch and sallies out to catch flying insects, as well as taking insects and spiders from foliage while hovering. Nest, usually in a fork of a small branch, is a neat cup of grasses, twigs, and plant fibers sometimes held together by spider webbing. The song, given frequently even in migration, is a sharp *che-bek*, often repeated as a rapid series. Call is a sharp *whit*.

Habitat

Common in mixed woodlands, parks, and orchards, usually in semi-open areas with brushy undergrowth. Winters from Mexico to Costa Rica, rarely in Florida.

Local Sites

The Least Flycatcher spends most of its day perched at the edge of a field or low in deciduous woods, constantly flicking its tail. Look for it during spring migration statewide.

FIELD NOTES Two look-alikes, Alder Flycatcher, *Empidonax alnorum* (inset) and Willow Flycatcher, *E. traillii*, were formerly classified as one species. They are best identified by voice: Alder says *fee-BE-o* and Willow says *FITZ-bew*. Both are larger than the Least and have less conspicuous eye rings.

Year-round | Adult

EASTERN PHOEBE

Sayornis phoebe L 7" (18 cm)

FIELD MARKS
Brownish gray above, darkest on head, wings, and tail; dark bill; lacks distinct wing bars

Underparts mostly white with pale olive wash on sides and breast

Fresh fall birds washed with yellow on belly

Behavior
Flicks tail constantly when perched, looking for flying insects to chase and snare in midair. Also easts small fish, berries, and fruit. Often builds delicate cup-like nest under bridges, in eaves, or in the rafters of old buildings, almost always near running water. Distinctive song is a rough, whistled *schree-dip,* followed by a descending *schree-brrr*, often repeated when male is attempting to lure a mate. Call is a sharp *tsip.*

Habitat
Found in woodlands, farmlands, and suburbs.

Local Sites
The Eastern Phoebe breeds statewide and is especially conspicuous during October durring migrating along coastal regions.

FIELD NOTES Though very similarly plumaged, the Eastern Phoebe is distinguished from the Eastern Wood-Pewee, *Contopus virens* (inset), by the phoebe's habit of constantly pumping its tail when perched. The wood-pewee tends to perch motionless. In addition, the wood-pewee's lower mandible is a dull orange, and it has two thin whitish wing bars.

Year-round | Adult

GREAT CRESTED FLYCATCHER

Myiarchus crinitus L 8" (20 cm)

FIELD MARKS

Gray face and breast contrasts
with bright yellow belly and
undertail coverts

Olive green above and on crest

Mostly rufous inner webs of
tail feathers

Behavior
Forages high in tall trees, picking insects from foliage
or snaging them in midair. During courtship, the male
chases the female near a chosen nesting cavity, which is
usually another bird's abandoned cavity or a birdbox.
Male rarely leaves a fertile female's side and defends
territory from other males in heated midair battles.
Leans forward and bobs head if agitated. Calls include
a loud, hoarse, ascending *whee-eep*, a softer *purr-it*,
and a series of *whit* notes. Sings a continuous series
of *whee-eep*s around dawn.

Habitat
Found in open deciduous and mixed woodlands,
including parks and suburbs. Winters for the most part
in Central and South America.

Local Sites
The Great Crested Flycatcher's *wheeep* call often betrays
its presence. Look for it during summer in your local
park or woodland, and during September on the coast.

FIELD NOTES The Great Crested Flycatcher has traditionally
decorated its nest with shed pieces of snakeskin, but these days
it will make do with cellophane, plastic wrap, and onion skins.

Year-round | Adult

EASTERN KINGBIRD

Tyrannus tyrannus L 8.5" (22 cm)

FIELD MARKS
Black head, slate gray back

White terminal band on black tail

Underparts white except for pale gray wash across breast

Orange-red crown patch visible only when displaying

Behavior
Waits on perch until it spots prey, then darts out to snare it in midair. Feeds primarily on flying insects. May also hover to pick food from foliage. Males court with erratic hovering, swooping, and circling, revealing hidden crown patch. Builds cup-shaped nest near the end of a tree branch, sometimes on a post or stump. Emits raspy *zeer* call when feeding or defending. Sings a complex, repeated series of notes and trills at dawn.

Habitat
Found in woodland clearings, farms, orchards, and field edges, usually near lakes, ponds and waterways. Winters in South America.

Local Sites
A familiar flycatcher that perches in the open, the Eastern Kingbird arrives late in the spring and leaves early in the fall. Look for it migrating along the coast during late August, when its numbers can be impressive.

FIELD NOTES Living up to its Latin name, which means "tyrant of tyrants," the Eastern Kingbird will actively defend its nest, sometimes pecking at and even pulling feathers from the backs of hawks, crows, and vultures.

Year-round | Adult

BLUE-HEADED VIREO

Vireo solitarius L 5" (13 cm)

FIELD MARKS

Solid blue-gray hood contrasts
with white spectacles and throat

Olive or bluish back; yellow sides
and flanks sometimes greenish

Prominent wing bars and tertial
edges; white on outer tail feathers

Behavior
Most often by itself or in a pair, the Blue-headed is the
first vireo to return to breeding grounds in spring. Forages on branches and treetops for insects and sometimes fruit. May also give chase to a flying insect or
hover to pick one off foliage. Courtship display involves
much singing, bobbing, and showcasing of yellow flank
feathers by the male. Nests in forks of trees or bushes.
Song, similar to the Red-eyed Vireo's, consists of short,
clear notes and is heard frequently throughout the day.

Habitat
Common in mixed woodlands at higher branches.

Local Sites
The sweet phrases of the Blue-headed Vireo's song are
the best indicator of its presence April through September, but it often stays high in the treetops offering only
fleeting views. Look for it in summer at Sapsucker
Woods in Ithaca and in fall migration along the coast,
foraging with warblers during September and October.

FIELD NOTES The Blue-headed Vireo was until 1997 grouped as a
single species, the Solitary Vireo, with two more westerly vireos,
now named the Plumbeous, *Vireo plumbeus*, and Cassin's, *Vireo
cassinii*. They were split primarily because a lack of overlap in
breeding ranges keeps these birds from frequently hybridizing.

Breeding | Adult

WARBLING VIREO

Vireo gilvus L 5.5" (14 cm)

FIELD MARKS

Gray to olive-gray above, whitish to yellowish below

Gray eye stripe, paler above eye

Blue-gray bill, legs, and feet

No wing bars; crown does not contrast with back

Behavior

Seen singly or in a pair, this bird's drab gray plumage can be hard to spot while perched near the tops of large trees. Forages slowly, deliberately, high in trees for insects, caterpillars, larvae, and sometimes fruit. Call is a harsh, nasal *gwee*. Song is a long, choppy warble of up to 20 notes, often ending in a down-slurred *buzz*. Male is known to sing even while incubating eggs.

Habitat

Found for the most part in wooded riparian areas of deciduous forests. Cup-shaped nest hangs between the fork of a tree, generally toward the end of a branch.

Local Sites

The Warbling Vireo can be heard in just about any patch of deciduous woodland from May through August. Look for it along the coast in September, where it occurs with mixed flocks of other migrants.

FIELD NOTES The Philadelphia Vireo, *Vireo philadelphicus* (inset), is very similar to the Warbling Vireo but is more olive, with a yellowish throat and a dark eye line extending to the bill. In New York it breeds primarily in the Adirondacks.

Year-round | Adult

RED-EYED VIREO

Vireo olivaceus L 6" (15 cm)

FIELD MARKS
Blue-gray crown

White eyebrow, bordered above
and below in black

Olive back, darker wings and tail

White underparts

Ruby red eye, visible at close range

Behavior
Searches through foliage for fruits, berries, and insects,
especially caterpillars. Sometimes hovers to snatch
food from high branches. Male known to chase female
during courtship, sometimes even pinning her to the
ground. Builds nest of grass and forest debris on horizontal tree limb. Song is a variable series of deliberate,
short phrases, *cheer-o-wit, cher-ee, chit-a wit, de-o*, sung
nearly nonstop from dawn through dusk and while
brooding, foraging, roosting, and even while
swallowing. Call is a whining, down-slurred *myahh*.

Habitat
Found in the forest canopies of deciduous woodlands.

Local Sites
The Red-eyed Vireo is a common breeder throughout
the state. Look and listen for it during the summer at a
local park or woodland—even in Central Park.

FIELD NOTES The Red-eyed Vireo's repetition of its monotonous
song for hours and hours without pausing has given it a wryly
humorous nickname, the Preacher Bird. In past centuries,
vireos have sometimes been called "greenlets"; the Latin word
Vireo refers to the color green, which some species show on
their upperparts.

Year-round | Adult

BLUE JAY

Cyanocitta cristata L 11" (28 cm)

FIELD MARKS

Blue crest and back

Black barring and white patches
on blue wings and tail

Black collar line on grayish white
underparts extends onto nape

Black bill, legs, and feet

Behavior
Often seen singly or in small family groups, foraging
for insects, acorns and other nuts, berries, and seeds.
Will also raid nests for eggs and nestlings of other
species. A bobbing display may be observed during
courtship. Builds nest in oak and beech trees 5 to 20
feet up. The noisy, bold Blue Jay gives a diverse array of
vocalizations, including a loud, piercing alarm call of
jay jay jay, a musical *yo-ghurt,* and imitations of several
hawk species, particularly the Red-shouldered Hawk.

Habitat
Found in fragmented woodlands, parks, and suburban
backyards. Some birds are migratory, while others are
year-round residents.

Local Sites
Blue Jays are common at feeders and in suburban backyards year-round. On the coast during October they are
conspicuous migrants in large numbers in some years.

FIELD NOTES A resourceful feeder, the Blue Jay will store acorns
in the ground for winter months when food is scarce. As many of
these acorns are never recovered, this practice is a major factor
in the establishment and distribution of oak forests throughout
the jay's range.

Year-round | Adult

AMERICAN CROW

Corvus brachyrhynchos L 17.5" (45 cm)

FIELD MARKS
Black, iridescent plumage overall
Broad wings and squared off tail
Long, heavy, black bill
Brown eyes
Black legs and feet

Behavior
Often forages, roosts, and travels in flocks. Individuals take turns at sentry duty while others feed on insects, garbage, grain, mice, eggs, and young birds. Known to noisily mob large raptors, such as eagles, hawks, and Great Horned Owls, in order to drive them from its territory. Because its bill is ineffective on tough hides, crows wait for another predator—or an automobile—to open a carcass before dining. Studies have shown the crow's ability to count, solve puzzles, and retain information. Nests in shrubs, trees, or on poles. Readily identified by its familiar *caw* call.

Habitat
One of North America's most widely distributed and familiar birds, lives in a variety of habitats.

Local Sites
Few species are as varied in habitat as this large "songbird," which is well-known to birders and nonbirders alike and common in forests, fields, towns, and cities.

FIELD NOTES The closely related and similarly plumaged Fish Crow, *Corvus ossifragus*, is smaller than the American Crow, but is best told apart by its high, nasal, two-syllable *unh-unh* call. It is increasing in both coastal and central New York.

Year-round | Adult male

HORNED LARK

Eremophila alpestris L 6.8-7.8" (17-20 cm)

FIELD MARKS

White or yellowish forehead bordered by black band, which ends in hornlike tufts on adult males

Black cheek stripes, bill, and bib

Yellow or white throat and underparts; brown or rufous upperparts

Behavior

The only lark native to North America forages on the ground mainly on seeds, grain, and some insects. The Horned Lark walks or runs, rather than hops, and it seldom alights on trees or bushes. Outside breeding season, these birds organize into flocks. Uses its bill and feet with long hind claws to create shallow depressions for nesting. Song begins with 2 or 3 *chit* notes, then flows into a rapid, jumbled twittering that rises slightly in pitch. Calls include a high-pitched *tsee-titi.*

Habitat

Found in open agricultural fields, grasslands, dirt fields, sod farms, airports, gravel ridges, and shores.

Local Sites

The Horned Lark is an inconspicuous breeder and a hardy winter resident in agricultural fields across the state and on coastal beaches.

FIELD NOTES The male Horned Lark performs a spectacular flight display, ascending several hundred feet, circling and singing for a bit, then plummeting headfirst toward the ground, flaring his wings open for landing at the last second. With horns upraised, he then struts for the female, having proven his aerial agility.

Year-round | Adult male

PURPLE MARTIN

Progne subis L 8" (20 cm)

FIELD MARKS

Male is dark, glossy purplish blue

Female has bluish gray upperparts; grayish breast and belly

Long, pointed wings; forked tail

Dark eyes, bill, legs, and feet

Juvenile brown above, gray below

Behavior
Forages almost exclusively in flight, darting for wasps,
bees, dragonflies, winged ants, and other large insects.
Long, sharply pointed wings and substantial tail allow
it graceful maneuverability in the air. Capable of
drinking, even bathing, in flight by skimming just over
water's surface and dipping bill, or breast, into water.
Nests almost exclusively in man-made multi-dwelling
martin houses. Song is a series of croaks and gurgles.

Habitat
Found in open areas near martin houses and water.
Winters in South America.

Local Sites
Spectacular concentrations of Purple Martins form
during late summer as the birds stage before migration.
Thousands may be present at Montezuma National
Wildlife Refuge in late August.

FIELD NOTES Purple Martins in eastern North America are highly
dependent on man-made nesting houses, which can hold many
pairs of breeding adults. The tradition of making martin houses
from hollowed gourds originated with Native Americans, who
found that this sociable bird helped reduce insects around vil-
lages and crops. The practice was adopted by colonists, and
martins have accordingly prospered for many generations.

Year-round | Adult

TREE SWALLOW

Tachycineta bicolor L 5.8" (15 cm)

FIELD MARKS

Dark, glossy, greenish blue above

White below

Slightly notched tail

Long, pointed, blackish wings

Juvenile gray-brown above with
dusky wash on its breast

Behavior

During migration, seen in huge flocks or perched in
long rows on branches and wires. Darts over fields or
water to catch insects in flight, but switches to diet of
berries and plant buds during colder months, when
insects are less abundant. Nests in tree cavities, fence
posts, barn eaves, and man-made birdhouses. Song is a
rapid, extended series of variable chirping notes—*chrit,
pleet, euree, cheet, chrit, pleet.*

Habitat

Found in wooded habitats near water, or where dead
trees provide nest holes in fields, marshes, or towns.

Local Sites

The most abundant and conspicuous swallow in the
state, the Tree Swallow is easy to find in summer in nest
boxes statewide and in fall migration along the coast,
where spectacular concentrations occur.

FIELD NOTES Among the world's swallows, the Tree Swallow
more regularly feeds on plant material and has a particular
fondness for waxy bayberries, for which it has developed a
special digesting ability. These adaptations allow it to migrate
north earlier than other swallows and linger later in the fall.

Year-round | Adult

Stelgidopteryx serripennis L 5" (13 cm)

FIELD MARKS

Plain brown above with darker
wings and slightly paler rump

White below with a brownish wash
on throat and breast

Juvenile has a rusty throat and
two cinnamon wing bars

Behavior

Mostly seen singly or in pairs, except in migration
when flocks form. Flies low over open fields and water,
snagging insects in flight. May also pick insects from
water's surface. Male suitor chases female during
courtship. Traditionally digs nesting burrows in
riparian areas, but has also adapted to cavities under
bridges and highway overpasses, and in drainage culverts, for nesting. Calls include a series of low-pitched,
upwardly inflected *brrt* notes, a buzzy *jrrr-jrrr-jrrr-jrrr*,
and a higher pitched *brzzzzzt*.

Habitat

Found in summer anywhere near water, especially
where steep banks of loose soil occur.

Local Sites

A common migrant in western New York, the Northern
Rough-winged Swallow also breeds statewide. Look for
flocks in August at Montezuma National Wildlife Refuge.

FIELD NOTES Often found breeding colonially in the
same exposed sandbanks as kingfishers and Northern Rough-wingeds, the Bank Swallow, *Riparia riparia*
(inset), is distinguished by its distinct brown breast
band. It also beats its wings more quickly than the
Northern Rough-winged as it flits about over its nesting tunnel, dug five to six feet into the sand.

Year-round | Adult

BARN SWALLOW

Hirundo rustica L 6.8" (17 cm)

FIELD MARKS
Long, deeply forked, dark tail

Iridescent deep blue upperparts;
cinnamon to whitish underparts,
paler on female

Rusty brown forehead and throat;
dark blue-black breast band

Behavior

An exuberant flyer, often seen in small flocks skimming
low over the surface of a field or pond, taking insects in
midair. Will follow tractors and lawn mowers to feed
on flushed insects. An indicator of coming storms, as
barometric pressure changes cause the bird to fly lower
to the ground. Has adapted to humans to the extent
that it now nests almost exclusively in structures such
as barns, bridges, culverts, and garages. Call in flight is
a high-pitched, squeaky *chee-jit*. Song is a long series of
squeaky warbles interrupted by nasal, grating rattles.

Habitat

Frequents open farms and fields, especially those near
water. Widely distributed all over the world.

Local Sites

Virtually every farm in the state hosts a colony of these
abundant swallows in barns and storage buildings
during the summer breeding season.

FIELD NOTES The Cliff Swallow, *Petrochelidon
pyrrhonota* (inset), can also be found in summer
nesting under bridges and eaves or foraging over
fields and ponds. In flight, it is best distinguished
from the Barn Swallow by its squarish tail and buffy
rump. Its pale forehead is a distinctive field mark as well.

Year-round | Adult

BLACK-CAPPED CHICKADEE

Poecile atricapillus L 5.3" (13 cm)

FIELD MARKS

Black cap and bib; white cheeks

Grayish upperparts

Whitish underparts with rich buffy flanks, more pronounced in fall

Wing feathers edged in white

Behavior

A common backyard bird, often the first to find a new bird feeder. Also forages along branches and probes bark of various trees. Diet varies seasonally, mostly insects in sumer, more seeds and berries in winter. Builds its nest in cavities in rotting wood or seeks out man-made nest box. Call sounds like *chick-a-dee-dee-dee.* Song is a variable, clear, whistled *fee-bee* or *fee-bee-ee,* the first note higher in pitch.

Habitat

Common in open woodlands, clearings, and suburbs.

Local Sites

The Black-capped Chickadee is the common breeding chickadee statewide and is a frequent feeder visitor in winter.

FIELD NOTES The Boreal Chickadee, *Poecile hudsonicus* (inset), has a dull brown cap, mostly-gray cheek, black bib, brownish back and rump, and rufous-brown or tawny flanks. It dwells in boreal forests across North America and reaches one of its southernmost breeding limits in the Adirondacks.

Year-round | Adult

TUFTED TITMOUSE

Baeolophus bicolor L 6.3" (16 cm)

FIELD MARKS

Gray above, whitish below

Russet wash on sides

Gray crest; blackish forehead

Pale spots around dark eyes

Juvenile has gray forehead and paler crest

Behavior

Very active forager in trees, seeking insects, spiders, snails, berries, and seeds. Known to hold a nut with its feet and pound it open with its bill. A common visitor to backyard feeders, especially fond of sunflower seeds and suet. Male feeds female in courtship. Nests in natural cavities, woodpecker holes, man-made boxes, and sometimes in fence posts. Song is a loud, whistled *peto-peto-peto* or *wheedle-wheedle-wheedle*. Employs up to ten different calls, including a harsh *zhee zhee zhee*, which it uses to keep foraging groups together.

Habitat

Found in open forests, woodlands, groves, and orchards, as well as urban and suburban parks.

Local Sites

Increasing in numbers, the Tufted Titmouse now occupies most of New York, absent only from mountains in the northeastern corner of the state. It is a common feeder visitor in winter.

FIELD NOTES Unintimidated by proximity to humans, the Tufted Titmouse will approach people who make a squeaking sound or *pish*, a useful tool for a birder. It is even known to swoop down and pluck hair directly from a human's scalp for use in its nest.

Year-round | Adult

WHITE-BREASTED NUTHATCH

Sitta carolinensis L 5.8" (15 cm)

FIELD MARKS
White face and breast; black cap

Blue-gray upperparts; wing and
tail feathers tipped in white

Rust or brown colored
underparts near legs

White pattern on blue-black tail

Behavior
Creeps down tree trunks or large branches in search of
insects and spiders. Will also gather nuts and seeds, jam
them into bark, and hammer or "hatch" the food open
with bill. Roosts in tree cavities, and sometimes even in
crevices of bark in summer. Builds nest in abandoned
woodpecker holes or in natural cavities inside decaying
trees. Song is a rapid series of nasal whistles on one
pitch: *whi-whi-whi-whi-whi-whi*. Call is a slow, low-
pitched, nasal *yank, yank*.

Habitat
Found in deciduous or mixed woods.

Local Sites
These upside-down tree climbers are present year-
round in large forests, small woodlands,
urban parks, and backyards throughout
the state.

FIELD NOTES In winter, the White-breasted often joins
mixed-species foraging groups with the Red-breasted
Nuthatch, *Sitta canadensis* (inset: female, top; male,
bottom). Though similar in behavior, the less
common Red-breasted is noticeably smaller
and has rust-colored underparts, darker on the males.
The Red-breasted forages on small branches and outer twigs.

Year-round | Adult

BROWN CREEPER

Certhia americana L 5.3" (13 cm)

FIELD MARKS
Mottled, streaky brown above

White eyebrow stripe

White underparts

Long, thin decurved bill

Long, graduated tail

Behavior
Camouflaged by streaked brown plumage, climbs upward from the base of a tree, then flies to a lower place on another tree in search of insects and larvae in tree bark. Long, decurved bill helps it to dig prey out of tree bark; its stiff tail feathers serving as a prop against the trunk. Forages by itself in general, unless part of a mixed-species flock in winter. Builds nests behind loose bark of dead or dying trees. Call is a soft, sibilant, almost inaudible *seee*. Song is a high-pitched *seee seeed-see sideeu*, or a similar variation.

Habitat
Found mostly in heavily forested areas. May wander into suburban and urban parks in winter.

Local Sites
The Brown Creeper is found year-round in woodlands throughout the state, but it is less numerous in winter. On the coast it can be a conspicuous fall migrant.

FIELD NOTES If the creeper suspects the presence of a predator, it will spread its wings and tail, press its body tight against the trunk of a tree, and remain completely motionless. In this pose, its camouflaged plumage makes it almost invisible.

Year-round | Adult

HOUSE WREN

Troglodytes aedon L 4.8" (12 cm)

FIELD MARKS
Grayish or brown upperparts

Fine black barring on wings
and tail

Pale gray underparts

Pale faint eye ring, eyebrow

Thin, slightly decurved bill

Behavior
Noisy, conspicuous, and relatively tame, with its tail
often cocked upward. Gleans insects and spiders from
vegetation. Forages at a variety of levels, including high
up in trees. Male begins construction on a number of
possible nests in any crevice of suitable size. Female
joins him, inspects the nests, and chooses one to complete. Sings exuberantly in a cascade of bubbling,
down-slurred trills. Call is a rough *chek-chek,* often
running into a chatter.

Habitat
Found in open woodlands and thickets, and in shrub-
bery around farms, parks, and suburban gardens.

Local Sites
Thickets, woodland edges, shrubby fields, and backyard
nesting boxes host breeding pairs throughout the state
in summer, especially in rural areas and small towns.

FIELD NOTES The Winter Wren, *Troglodytes troglodytes* (inset), has a
short, stubby tail and darker barring on its belly than the House
Wren. Its song is a rapid series of melodious
trills, and its sharp *chimp-chimp* call is distinctive. The secretive Winter Wren nests in dense
brush, especially along stream banks in
moist, coniferous woods.

Year-round | Adult male

RUBY-CROWNED KINGLET

Regulus calendula L 4.2" (11 cm)

FIELD MARKS

Olive green above; dusky below

Yellow-edged plumage on wings

Two white wing bars

Short black bill; white eye ring

Male's red crown patch seldom
visible except when agitated

Behavior

Often seen foraging in mixed-species flocks, the Ruby-
crowned Kinglet flicks its wings frequently as it
searches for insects and their eggs or larvae on tree
trunks, branches, and foliage. May also give chase to
flying insects or drink sap from tree wells drilled by
sapsuckers. Calls include a scolding *ji-dit;* song consists
of several high, thin *tsee* notes, followed by descending
tew notes, ending with a trilled three-note phrase.

Habitat

Common in coniferous and mixed woodlands and
brushy thickets. Highly migratory.

Local Sites

The Ruby-crowned Kinglet breeds in the Adirondacks
at high elevations, but it is most easily observed as a fall
migrant on the coast in late October.

FIELD NOTES The Golden-crowned Kinglet,
Regulus satrapa (inset), is set apart by its yellow crown patch and its white eyebrow. The
male (inset, bottom) shows a brilliant orange
tuft within his yellow crown patch.

Year-round | Adult male

EASTERN BLUEBIRD

Sialia sialis L 7" (18 cm)

FIELD MARKS

Male is bright blue above

Female is a grayer blue above, duller below

Chestnut throat, breast, flanks, and sides of neck

White belly and undertail coverts

Behavior

Hunts from elevated perch in the open, dropping to the ground to seize crickets, grasshoppers, and spiders. Has been observed pouncing on prey it has spotted from as many as 130 feet away. In winter, forms small flocks and roosts communally at night in tree cavities or nest boxes. During courtship, male shows vivid coloring on his side during wing-waving displays beside a chosen nesting site. Nests in woodpecker holes, hollow trees or stumps, and in nest boxes. Call is a musical, rising *too-lee*, extended in song to *too too-lee too-lee.*

Habitat

Found in open woodlands, meadows with scattered trees, farmlands, and orchards.

Local Sites

Present year-round, the Eastern Bluebird is most easily found during spring and summer breeding in nest boxes in open meadow habitat. It is sometimes a common migrant along the coast in November.

FIELD NOTES The Eastern Bluebird's serious decline in decades past is due largely to competition for nesting sites with two introduced species, the European Starling (pages 188-9), and the House Sparrow (pages 260-1). Specially designed bluebird nesting boxes provided by concerned birders have contributed to a promising comeback.

Year-round | Adult

HERMIT THRUSH

Catharus guttatus L 6.8" (17cm)

FIELD MARKS

Gray-brown upperparts; white to buffy underparts with dense spotting mostly on breast

Reddish tail contrasts with upperparts

Whitish eye ring; dark lateral throat streak

Behavior

A shy, terrestrial bird that forages on the forest floor for insects or in bushes in search of berries. If interrupted, it flies up into a low bush, flicking its wings nervously and slowly raising and lowering its tail. Common call is a blackbird-like *chuck*, often doubled; song is a serene series of clear, flutelike notes, the phrases repeated at different pitches, lending it a lyrical quality.

Habitat

For breeding, coniferous forests typically in areas of relatively little undergrowth. In winter and migration uses a wide variety of habitats, especially shady areas of river valleys. always with forest or brushy cover nearby.

Local Sites

In summer the haunting song of the Hermit Thrush can be heard from deep within woodlands, especially at high elevations. Listen for it at Ferd's Bog near the village of Inlet in the Adirondacks, and see it as a common fall migrant along the coast in October.

FIELD NOTES The Swainson's Thrush, *Catharus ustulatus* (inset), is spot-breasted like the Hermit Thrush but differs by its bold, buffy eye ring, olive-and-buffy face pattern, and its olive tail. It sings an ascending series of soft, liquid whistles.

Year-round | Adult

WOOD THRUSH

Hylocichla mustelina L 7.8" (20 cm)

FIELD MARKS
Reddish brown above, brightest
on crown and nape

White face and chest streaked
and spotted in black

Rump and tail brownish olive

White eye ring

Behavior
Feeds on the ground or close to it, foraging for insects,
spiders, fruits, and berries. Known to rub ants on its
feathers while preening. During courtship, male chases
female in quick, circling flight. Best known for its loud,
liquid song of three- to five-note phrases, each usually
ending with a trilled whistle, which can be heard in
summer before daybreak or at dusk. Calls include a
rapid *pit-pit-pit* and a rolling *popopopo*.

Habitat
Found in moist, shaded undergrowth of deciduous or
mixed woods, and seldom seen outside of dense forest.

Local Sites
A familiar breeding bird in mature forests and wooded
suburban areas, the Wood Thrush is notable for its
song heard from May through July at dawn and dusk.
Not observed in large numbers as a migrant, this
species is most easily found by listening for its song.

FIELD NOTES The Veery, *Catharus fuscescens* (inset), is slightly
smaller than the Wood Thrush, but is white below with gray
flanks, a grayish face, and an indistinct and
incomplete gray eye ring. Its upperparts are reddish brown from crown to tail, and its breast is less
spotted. Its song is a descending series of *veer*
notes, and its call is a sharp, descending, whistled *veer*, giving rise to its name.

Year-round | Adults

AMERICAN ROBIN

Turdus migratorius L 10" (25 cm)

FIELD MARKS
Brick red underparts, paler in
female, spotted in juvenile

Brownish gray above with darker
head and tail

White throat and lower belly

Broken white eye ring; yellow bill

Behavior
Best known and largest of the thrushes, often seen on
suburban lawns, hopping about and cocking its head
in search of earthworms. Gleans butterflies, damselflies,
and other flying insects from foliage and sometimes
takes prey in flight. Robins also eat fruit, especially in
fall and winter. This broad plant and animal diet makes
them one of the most successful and wide-ranging
thrushes. Nests in shrubs, trees, and even on sheltered
windowsills. Calls include a low, mellow *pup*, a doubled
or tripled *chok* or *tut*, and a sharp *kli ki ki ki ki*. Song is
a clear, variable *cheerily cheery cheerily cheery*.

Habitat
Common and widespread, forages on lawns and in
woodlands. Winters mostly near thickets, woodland
edges, and urban parks rich in fruit-bearing trees.

Local Sites
Look for the American Robin in any backyard. The
species is everywhere, including the most crowded
big cities.

FIELD NOTES The juvenile robin, which can be seen every year
between May and September, has a paler breast, like the female
of the species, but its underparts are heavily spotted with brown.
Look as well for the buff fringes on its back and wing feathers
and its short, pale buff eyebrow.

Year-round | Adult

NORTHERN MOCKINGBIRD

Mimus polyglottos L 10" (25 cm)

FIELD MARKS
Gray overall; darker above

White wing patches and outer tail feathers flash conspicuously in flight

Long, blackish wings and tail

Short, black bill

Behavior

The pugnacious Northern Mockingbird will protect its territory against other birds as well as dogs, cats, and humans. Has a varied diet that includes berries, grasshoppers, spiders, snails, and earthworms. An expert mimic, the mockingbird is known for its variety of songs, learning and imitating calls of many other species and animals. Typically repeats a song's phrases three times before beginning a new one. Often sings at night during nesting season. Call is a loud, sharp *check.*

Habitat

Resides in a variety of habitats, including cities, towns, and suburbs.

Local Sites

A familiar resident of edge and suburban habitats, the Northern Mockingbird often perches in the open atop a shrub or hedgerow. It is easily found in lowland habitat near the coast.

FIELD NOTES The Northern Mockingbird in flight (inset) reveals conspicuous white patches on its wings and outer tail feathers. While hunting, it shows these same white patches in a wing-flashing display that perhaps serves to startle insects into the open.

Year-round | Adult

BROWN THRASHER

Toxostoma rufum L 11.5" (29 cm)

FIELD MARKS

Reddish brown above

Pale buff to white below with heavy dark streaking

Long, reddish brown tail

Yellow eyes; dark, decurved bill

Two white wing bars

Behavior

Forages through leaf litter for insects, fruit, and grain; finds additional prey by digging with decurved bill. Courtship involves little fanfare, the whole process consisting of one or both birds picking up leaves or twigs and dropping them in front of the other. Nests in bushes, on ground, or in low trees. Sings from an exposed perch a long series of varied melodious phrases, each one given two or three times. Calls include a loud, smacking *spuck* and a low *churr*.

Habitat

Found in hedgerows, dense brush, and woodland edges.

Local Sites

The Brown Thrasher, a less conspicuous breeder than its cousin, the Northern Mockingbird (preceding pages), is most easily found along the coast during fall migration in September and October. Listen for its hard *chek* call from deep thickets.

FIELD NOTES Sharing the Northern Mockingbird's talent for mimicking the songs of other birds, the Gray Catbird, *Dumetella carolinensis* (inset), is most readily identified by its harsh, descending *mew* call. Plain dark gray with a black cap and a long, black tail, often cocked. Its undertail coverts are chestnut.

Nonbreeding | Adult

EUROPEAN STARLING

Sturnus vulgaris L 8.5" (22 cm)

FIELD MARKS

Iridescent black breeding plumage

Buffy tips on back, tail feathers

Fall feathers tipped in white,
giving speckled appearance

Yellow bill in summer; its base is
pale blue on male, pink on female

Behavior

A social and aggressive bird, feeds on a variety of food,
ranging from invertebrates—such as snails, worms, and
spiders—to fruit, berries, grains, seeds, and garbage.
Probes ground, opening bill to create small holes and
expose prey. Usually seen in flocks, except while nesting
in cavities, ranging from crevices in urban settings to
woodpecker holes and nest boxes. Imitates calls of
other species and emits high-pitched notes, including
squeaks, hisses, whistles, rattles, and wheezes.

Habitat

The adaptable starling thrives in a variety of habitats
near humans, including urban centers and farmland.

Local Sites

Big cities, towns, and farmlands are all home to this
ubiquitous import from Europe. Look for immense
flocks that gather during early fall and winter.

FIELD NOTES A Eurasian species introduced into New York's
Central Park in 1890, the European Starling has since spread
throughout the U.S. and Canada. Abundant, bold, and aggressive, starlings often compete for and take over nest sites of
native birds, including bluebirds, Wood Ducks, a variety of
woodpeckers, Tree Swallows, and Purple Martins.

Year-round | Adult

CEDAR WAXWING

Bombycilla cedrorum L 7.3" (19 cm)

FIELD MARKS

Distinctive sleek crest

Black mask bordered in white

Brownish head, back, breast, and
sides; pale yellow belly; gray rump

Yellow terminal tail band

May have red, waxy tips on wings

Behavior

Eats the most fruit of any North American bird. Up to
84% of its diet are cedar, holly, and hawthorn berries
and crabapple fruit. Also eats sap, flower petals, and
insects. Moves long distances only when food sources
run out. Gregarious in nature, waxwings band together
for foraging and protection. Flocks containing several
to a few hundred birds may feed side by side in winter,
then rapidly disperse, startling potential predators. Call
is a high-pitched, trilled *zeeeee*.

Habitat

Found in a variety of open habitats wherever fruit and
berries are available.

Local Sites

The handsome Cedar Waxwing is rather unpredictable
in its movements, but it is common along the coast
during migration. In winter it forages on berries in
mixed flocks with American Robins.

FIELD NOTES One of the more courteous diners in the bird world,
Cedar Waxwings have been known to perch side by side and pass
a piece of food down the row, one bird to the next, until one of them
decides to eat it. If the bird at the end of the line receives the morsel
and is disinclined as well, it is passed right back up the line.

Year-round | Adult male

BLUE-WINGED WARBLER

Vermivora pinus L 4.8" (12 cm)

FIELD MARKS

Male has bright yellow crown and underparts; female duller

Blue-gray wings with two white wing bars

Black eye line

White underside of tail

Behavior

Forages low to the ground for insects and spiders. May hover briefly while probing foliage with long, slender bill. Nests on or near the ground at the base of a shrub or in a clump of grass. Readily hybridizes with Golden-winged Warbler (inset, below). Frequently given call is a gentle *tsip*; also gives a high, *tzii* in flight. Songs are high-pitched, buzzy: *beeee-bzzzz* or *be-ee-ee-ee-btttt*.

Habitat

Found in overgrown fields, open brushy woodland edges, and in thickets. Winters in Central America.

Local Sites

The Blue-winged Warbler is increasing and replacing the Golden-winged Warbler in much of the state. Look for migrants in May and in August through September along the coast, especially at Muttontown Preserve in central Long Island.

FIELD NOTES The Golden-winged Warbler, *Vermivora chrysoptera* (inset: female, top; male, bottom), is declining largely due to hybridization with and displacement by the Blue-winged. The Golden-winged shows a yellow forecrown, a striking face pattern, and extensive yellow on the wings. Hybrids show a variety of intermediate characteristics.

Year-round | Adult male

YELLOW WARBLER

Dendroica petechia L 5" (13 cm)

FIELD MARKS

Bright yellow overall

Plump and short-tailed

Dark eye prominent in yellow face

Male shows distinct reddish streaks below; streaks faint or absent in female

Behavior

Mostly seen alone or in a pair. Forages in trees, shrubs, and bushes, gleaning insects, larvae, and fruit from branches and leaves. Will sometimes spot flying insects from a perch and chase them down. Nests in the forks of trees or bushes at eye level or a little higher. Male and female both feed nestlings. Habitually bobs tail and is quite vocal. Call is a husky, downslurred *tchip* or a thinner *tsip*. Primary song is a rapid, variable *sweet sweet sweet sweeter than sweet*. Alternate songs are longer and more complex.

Habitat

Favors wet habitats, especially near willows and alders; also found in open woodlands, gardens, and orchards.

Local Sites

The Yellow Warbler breeds commonly across the state and migrates along the coast in August and September.

FIELD NOTES The Yellow Warbler is notable for its efforts to thwart nest-parasitic Brown-headed Cowbirds (pages 252-3) by covering alien cowbird eggs with a new floor in the nest and laying a new clutch of its own eggs on top.

Breeding | Adult male

CHESTNUT-SIDED WARBLER

Dendroica pensylvanica L 5" (13 cm)

FIELD MARKS

Breeding male has yellow crown;
black eye and malar stripes;
chestnut sides

Female has greenish crown and
less chestnut

Two yellowish wing bars; black-
streaked back

Behavior

An active forager, often drooping its wings and cocking
its tail above its back, gleans insects, caterpillars, seeds,
and berries from low foliage or directly from ground.
May sometimes take insects in flight. Nest of grass,
sticks, and roots located near the ground in shrubby
understory. Call is a loud, sweet *chip*. Male sings conspicuously from exposed perch a whistled *please, please,
pleased to meetcha* or a *wee-weewee-wee-chi-tee-wee*.

Habitat

Breeds in open brushy woodlands, especially second-
growth deciduous ones, and in overgrown fields.
Found in a variety of woodlands during migration.

Local Sites

Lindsay-Parsons Biodiversity Preserve near Ithaca is a
good place to look for breeding Chestnut-sided
Warblers. They are also easily found as coastal migrants
in September.

FIELD NOTES During fall migration, which peaks in
early September, immatures (inset) look very different. They are lime green above and whitish
below, with a gray face and a distinct white eye
ring. Adult males retain dull chestnut sides.

Breeding | Adult male

MAGNOLIA WARBLER

Dendroica magnolia L 5" (13 cm)

FIELD MARKS

Yellow below, heavily streaked in black; blue-gray above with blackish and olive patches

White subterminal band on tail

Breeding male has broad black eye line and white eyebrow

Behavior
Forages alone or in a pair, gleaning insects, larvae, caterpillars, and spiders from branches and leaves. Fans its tail frequently, revealing black-and-white tail pattern. Nests close to the ground in a conifer. Calls include a high-pitched *enk*, given often in fall migration, and a high, buzzy *zee*, given in flight. Males sings from conspicuous perch a variable, short, musical *weeta weeta wit-chew* or an unaccented *sing sweet.*

Habitat
Breeds in cool, damp coniferous and mixed woods at high elevations. Especially associated with hemlocks.

Local Sites
The Magnolia Warbler breeds at Summer Hill State Forest and many other woodlands at relatively high elevations. It can be found easily in September migrating along the coast.

FIELD NOTES Though the Magnolia Warbler's breeding haunts are in northern forests, the species was named incongruously by the great ornithologist Alexander Wilson. The bird he officially described to science was a migrant he found in a magnolia tree in Mississippi.

Year-round | Adult male

BLACK-THROATED BLUE WARBLER

Dendroica caerulescens L 5.3" (13 cm)

FIELD MARKS

Male is dark blue above, white below, with black face, throat, and sides

Female is brownish above, buffy below, with pale eyebrow

White patch at base of primaries is smaller on female

Behavior

Seen alone or in a pair, which is the easiest way to identify the female. Forages fairly low in trees and brush for insects and larvae; also feeds on fruit and tree sap during migration. Builds nest with various plant materials in the fork of a low shrub or sapling. Calls include a popping *tuk* and a prolonged *tseet* in flight. Primary song is a slow series of buzzy notes, rising at the end: *zhee zhee zhee zeeee.*

Habitat

Breeds in high-elevation hardwood forests with thick shrubby underbrush. Found in a variety of woods and shrubby areas in migration. Males and females winter separately on a number of Caribbean islands.

Local Sites

Ferd's Bog is a good place to find breeding birds. Look for migrants along the coast in September.

FIELD NOTES The Cerulean Warbler, *Dendroica cerulea* (inset: male), is another largely blue wood-warbler in New York. The male is sky blue above and white below, with black streaking on his sides and breast. The female is bluish gray above with a buffy breast and throat and a whitish eyebrow. This species nests high in deciduous trees, and tends to stay high, making it quite a challenge to spot one.

Immature | "Myrtle"

YELLOW-RUMPED WARBLER

Dendroica coronata L 5.3" (13 cm)

FIELD MARKS
Bright yellow rump; yellow patch on sides of breast; pale eyebrow; white throat and sides of neck

Winter birds grayish brown above, white below with brown streaking

Breeding birds have yellow patch on crown, grayish blue upperparts

Behavior
Easily located and observed darting about for insects and spiders in the spring and summer; for myrtle berries and seeds in fall and winter. Eastern subspecies is named "Myrtle" Warbler because of its highly preferred winter food, berries of the myrtle or bayberry. Courtship involves intensive singing—a clear warble and a musical trill. Nest typically on a horizontal conifer branch. Nest building, incubation carried out mainly by the female.

Habitat
Common breeder in coniferous and mixed woodlands, primarily at high elevations; common to abundant in migration and winter on barrier beaches and, increasingly, in wooded and brushy areas inland.

Local Sites
Ferd's Bog is a good location to see the Yellow-rumped Warbler in the spring. It migrates in large numbers along the coast during October and November.

FIELD NOTES In the spring look for the male Yellow-rumped Warbler's bright breeding plumage (inset), characterized by a yellow crown patch and grayish blue upperparts. The female has a smaller crown patch and dusky brown upperparts.

Year-round | Adult male

BLACK-THROATED GREEN WARBLER

Dendroica virens L 5" (13 cm)

FIELD MARKS
Yellow face with greenish ear patch; greenish upperparts

Blackish wings with two white wing bars; whitish below

Male has black throat, upper breast, and streaks on its flanks; female has less black

Behavior
Tends to forage away from the tips of branches at about mid-level, gleaning insects, larvae, and some berries while in migration. Builds nest of grasses, plants, and stems in fork of a deciduous tree or, less frequently, a conifer. Calls: a soft, flat *tsip* and a high, sweet *see*. Song given near nest to attract mate is a variable, whistled, buzzy *zee-zee-zee-zoo-zee*. Territorial song to ward off other males is a more deliberate *zoo zee zoo zoo zee*.

Habitat
Breeds primarily in hardwood forests, sometimes also in mixed woods. Found in a variety of wooded and brushy areas during migration.

Local Sites
A fairly common breeder in coniferous forests in much of the state. In migration it is common in May at Derby Hill on Lake Ontario; look for it as well along the coast in September and October.

FIELD NOTES Wood-warblers number about 116 species, 57 in North America, over 30 of which frequent the East. North American wood-warblers have undergone significant recent declines, resulting chiefly from habitat destruction. Since most species migrate to the tropics they are at risk there and along their migration route as well. Many species' winter ranges are smaller than their breeding ranges, which amplifies the danger.

Breeding | Adult male

BLACKBURNIAN WARBLER

Dendroica fusca L 5" (13 cm)

FIELD MARKS

Male has distinctive orange and
black facial pattern; black above
with extensive white patches

Female and fall male: paler yellow
on throat

White belly and undertail coverts;
sides streaked with black

Behavior

Tends to remain at the treetops, gleaning insects,
caterpillars, and berries from foliage and twigs. Solitary
and territorial during nesting period, but will forage
with other species such as chickadees, kinglets, and
nuthatches after nestlings fledge. Calls include a rich
tsip and a buzzy *zzee* in flight. Primary song is a high-
pitched, ascending series of notes, ending with an
almost inaudible trill: *see-see-see-see-ti-ti-ti-siiii.*

Habitat

Stays mostly in the upper branches of coniferous and
mixed forests while breeding. Found in a variety of
woodlands and woodland edges during migration.

Local Sites

The handsome Blackburnian Warbler can be heard
and seen easily along the Lake Ontario shoreline as
a migrant in late May. On the coast it is a regular
fall migrant.

FIELD NOTES Like other juvenile warblers, young Blackburnians
will follow their parents while they forage and beg for food with
noisy *chip* notes. Immatures show a dark ear patch outlined in
drab yellow and a greenish forehead with a distinctive patch of
pale yellow. Look also for the yellowish streaks on their backs.

Year-round | Adult male

PRAIRIE WARBLER

Dendroica discolor L 4.8" (12 cm)

FIELD MARKS

Bright yellow below with black streaks on sides

Olive above; faint chestnut streaks on back, more visible on male

Bright yellow above and below eye; black line through and below eyes on male

Behavior

A very active bird, it constantly pumps its tail while foraging for insects and spiders on bushes, low tree branches, or the ground. Generally solitary or in a pair, but joins mixed flocks on migration. Sings from exposed perch its distinctive song, a rising series of buzzy *zee* notes. Call is a rich, full *chick*.

Habitat

Open second-growth woodlands, especially ones with pines, scrublands, and overgrown fields, but not prairies (it was misnamed when first found). Cup-shaped nest is hidden in trees or bushes.

Local Sites

The Prairie Warbler is a common breeder in the southeastern portion of the state and is expanding its range. It breeds in the piney woods at the eastern end of Long Island and migrates along the coast in September.

FIELD NOTES A frequent host of the Brown-headed Cowbird's (pages 252-3) nest parasitism, the Prairie Warbler is becoming even more vulnerable as its habitat is further restricted by development. Since it raises only two broods each year, even if one is jeopardized by the cowbird's egg-dropping, the future of this species may depend upon careful land management.

Breeding | Adult male

BLACK-AND-WHITE WARBLER

Mniotilta varia L 5.3" (13 cm)

FIELD MARKS

Boldly striped on head, most of
body, and undertail coverts

Male's throat and cheeks are
black in breeding plumage;
in winter, chin is white

Females and immatures have
pale cheeks

Behavior
The only warbler that creeps around branches and up
and down tree trunks, foraging like a nuthatch. Probes
crevices in the bark of trees with its long bill for insects,
caterpillars, and spiders. Song is a long series of high,
thin *wee-see* notes; calls include a sharp *chip* and a high
seep-seep. If disturbed at nest, female drags wings on
the ground with tail spread for distraction.

Habitat
Prefers forests, both deciduous and mixed woodlands,
as well as forested margins of swamps and rivers. Nests
on the ground, close to the base of a bush or tree, or in
the hollow of a stump or log.

Local Sites
The Black-and-white Warbler is a common migrant
and breeder in woodlands statewide. Look for it along
the Lake Ontario shoreline in spring and along the
coast during fall.

FIELD NOTES The Black-and-white Warbler was once referred
to as the Black-and-white Creeper because of its creeper- or
nuthatch-like feeding behavior. This species returns to its northern breeding grounds about two weeks earlier than most other
warblers; it can feed on insects in bark crevices before tree
leaves have developed.

Year-round | Adult male

AMERICAN REDSTART

Setophaga ruticilla L 5.3" (13 cm)

FIELD MARKS

Male is glossy black above and on hood; bright orange patches on sides, wings, and tail

Female gray-olive above; orange patches replaced with yellow

White belly and undertail coverts

Behavior

Often fans tail and spreads wings when perched. Darts suddenly to snare flying insects. Also takes insects, caterpillars, spiders, berries, fruit, and seeds from branches and foliage. Nests in forks of trees or bushes generally 10 to 20 feet from the ground. Song is a highly variable series of high, thin notes usually followed by a single, wheezy, downslurred note: *zee zee zee zee zweeah*. Calls include a thin, squeaky *chip* and a clear, penetrating *seep* in flight.

Habitat

The American Redstart is found in moist deciduous and mixed woodlands with thick undergrowth; also in wooded riparian zones and second-growth woodlands.

Local Sites

A common migrant and breeder in most of the state; look for them even in Central Park. It is especially common along the coast in September and October, at "migrant traps" such as Jones Beach.

FIELD NOTES The female American Redstart (inset) shows yellow patches wherever the male shows orange, except in some older females who have acquired an orange cast to their plumage. Females are further set apart by a light gray head and an olive-green back. Immature males resemble females, but with some black spotting on their lores and breast.

Year-round | Adult on nest

OVENBIRD

Seiurus aurocapilla L 6" (15 cm)

FIELD MARKS

Russet crown bordered in black

Olive-brown above, white below
with dark brown streaks

Brown malar stripe, white chin

Bold white eye ring

Pinkish bill and legs

Behavior
Typically seen on the ground; walks rather than hops;
tail cocked, wings dropped, and head bobbing. Forages
among leaves and twigs for insects, caterpillars, earthworms, snails, seeds, fruit, and berries. Known to kick
up leaf litter to expose prey, a strategy more commonly
employed by sparrows than warblers. Nests on the
ground in small depression covered with grasses and
leaves and entered on the side, resembling a tiny dutch
oven (pictured, opposite). Primary song is a loud,
ascending *TEA-cher TEA-cher TEA-cher*. Calls include a
loud, sharp *tsick*, given rapidly if alarmed, and a high,
thin *seee* in flight. Also gives an elaborate flight song.

Habitat
Found in mature hardwood, deciduous, and mixed
forests, where it stays primarily in thick undergrowth.

Local Sites
The Ovenbird can be heard, more often than seen, in
forests statewide. It is also a common migrant along the
Lake Ontario shoreline in May and along the coast during September and October.

FIELD NOTES Ovenbirds are often easy to hear as the song of one
male will invariably elicit a response from a neighboring male,
producing a domino effect until the woods resonate with their
competing melodies.

Year-round | Adult

NORTHERN WATERTHRUSH

Seiurus noveboracensis L 5.8" (15 cm)

FIELD MARKS

Long, narrow, buffy eyebrow

Plain brown upperparts; buffy, heavily streaked underparts

Long, dull-pinkish legs

Behavior
The hallmark of a waterthrush is its teetering walk. It constantly bobs its rear end and tail as it forages along the water's edge, turning over leaves and litter in search of insects and other small invertebrates. The Northern Waterthrush may even walk in shallow water. Its nest is an open cup combining many kinds of plant material placed in a stump, under a bank, or in roots of a fallen tree. Song is a loud, three-part series of triplets descending in pitch: *twit-twit-twit, sweet-sweet-sweet, chew-chew-chew.* Call is a ringing *chink.*

Habitat
Woodlands with still or slow-moving water, particularly swamps, bogs, and edges of lakes. Winters from Mexico and the Caribbean south to central South America.

Local Sites
Breeds in suitable habitat in most of the state; Ithaca's Sapsucker Woods is a good place to look. It is common on the coast during migration in September.

FIELD NOTES The Louisiana Waterthrush, *Seiurus motacilla* (inset), prefers fast-moving woodland streams in contrast to the Northern Waterthrush's preferred calm wetlands. Identify the Louisiana by its bold, white supercilium, wider behind the eye.

Year-round | Adult male

CANADA WARBLER

Wilsonia canadensis L 5.3" (13 cm)

FIELD MARKS

Male unmistakable: dark gray upperparts; prominent yellow spectacles; black necklace on yellow breast

Female and immature: duller; necklace indistinct or absent

Behavior

A lively forager, the Canada Warbler frequently darts out from trees and bushes like a flycatcher to catch insects in flight. It also captures insects and spiders on foliage in the typical warbler manner. Nest is a loose cup of dead leaves, grasses, and other plant material on or near the ground, often on a mossy log, stump, or roots of a fallen tree. Song typically opens with a sharp *chip* and continues with a loud series of varied clear, chipping, sputtering, and warbling notes. Call is a sharp *chup*.

Habitat

Fairly common in cool, moist woodlands with dense undergrowth, and in bogs and swamps. Winters in South America.

Local Sites

In late May look for the striking Canada Warbler as a migrant in Central Park. It breeds throughout the state at higher elevations.

FIELD NOTES Aptly named for its gray hood, the Mourning Warbler, *Oporornis philadelphia* (inset: female, left; male, right) breeds in dense undergrowth in woodland clearings, marshy bottomlands, forest roadsides, and utility right-of-ways. Singing its loud *cheery-cheery-cheery, chorry-chorry,* it is more often heard than seen.

Year-round | Adult male

COMMON YELLOWTHROAT

Geothlypis trichas L 5" (13 cm)

FIELD MARKS

Adult male shows broad, black
mask bordered above by light gray

Female lacks black mask, has
whitish patch around eyes

Grayish olive upperparts; bright
yellow throat and breast; pale
yellow undertail coverts

Behavior

Generally remains close to the ground, skulking and
hiding in undergrowth. May also be seen climbing vertically on stems and singing from exposed perches.
While foraging, cocks tail and hops on ground to glean
insects, caterpillars, and spiders from foliage, twigs, and
reeds. Nests atop piles of weeds and grass, or in small
shrubs. One version of variable song is a loud, rolling
wichity wichity wichity wichity wich. Calls include a
husky *tshep*, a rapid chatter, and a buzzy *dzip* in flight.

Habitat

Stays low in marshes, shrubby fields, woodland edges,
and thickets near water.

Local Sites

The familiar warbler can be found breeding anywhere
its preferred habitat occurs. It is especially common
along the coast during fall migration. Look for it at
Fire Island during late September.

FIELD NOTES The largest North American
warbler at 7.5", the Yellow-breasted
Chat, *Icteria virens* (inset: male), is also an
elusive skulker. Like the Yellowthroat, it
remains low to the ground, hidden in dense vegetation. Listen for its harsh, jumbled, unmusical
song, given from a perch or in flight.

Breeding | Adult male

SCARLET TANAGER

Piranga olivacea L 7" (18 cm)

FIELD MARKS

Breeding male has bright red body and black wings and tail; 1st spring male has browner wings

Female is olive above with darker wings and tail; yellow below

Fall adult male resembles female

Behavior

Forages for insects, berries, and fruit mostly high in the tops of trees, but will also take food from the ground or snag insects on the fly. The Scarlet Tanager's courtship display consists of a male perching below a prospective mate and spreading his wings to reveal his scarlet back. Male's song is robinlike but raspier, given to defend territory and attract a mate: *querit queer querry querit queer*. Female sings a similar song, but softer and shorter. Call is a hoarse *chip* or *chip-burr*.

Habitat

This resident of the forest interior is found in almost any mature woodland that is not heavily fragmented.

Local Sites

Breeds throughout the state and is a common migrant during spring and fall. The coast in late September is a good place to see migrants; singing males in Central Park are quite a sight in May.

FIELD NOTES The female Scarlet Tanager (inset) is easily set apart from the breeding male by olive upperparts and yellow underparts, but the male molts into a similar plumage after breeding. Note his darker wings and tail. In late summer, you may even find a male in mid-molt with green, yellow, and red splotches.

Year-round | Adult male

EASTERN TOWHEE

Pipilo erythrophthalmus L 7.5" (19 cm)

FIELD MARKS
Male has black hood, upperparts
Female similarly patterned, but black areas replaced by brown
Rufous sides; white underparts
White corners on long tail
Juvenile streaked light brown

Behavior
Stays low to the ground, scratching leaf litter frequently with feet together, head held low and tail up, exposing insect prey and seeds. Also forages for grasshoppers, spiders, moths, and fruit. Male fans his wings and tail during courtship, displaying contrasting white patches on his primaries and tertials. Nests on the ground, near shrubs. Sings from an exposed perch a loud, ringing *drink your tea*, sometimes shortened to *drink tea*. Also calls in an emphatic, upslurred *chewink*.

Habitat
The Eastern Towhee prefers second-growth woodlands with dense shrubs, brushy thickets, and extensive leaf litter. Also found in brambly fields, suburban hedgerows, riparian areas, and forest clearings.

Local Sites
Occupies shrubby habitats statewide. It is a common migrant along the coast, where it can be found April through May and September through October.

FIELD NOTES The juvenile Eastern Towhee (inset) has a brown cap, wings, and tail, and is heavily streaked with brown, which is especially distinct on its buff underparts. Look for it only in summer; the molt into full adult colors takes place in its first fall.

Breeding | Adult

CHIPPING SPARROW

Spizella passerina L 5.5" (14 cm)

FIELD MARKS

Breeding adult shows bright
chestnut crown, white eyebrow,
gray cheek and nape

Winter adult has streaked brown
crown and a brown face

Streaked brown wings and back;
unstreaked gray breast and belly

Behavior

Forages on the ground for insects, caterpillars, spiders,
and seeds. May be found foraging in small family flocks
in late summer. Along with the related Field Sparrow
(p. 229) and American Tree Sparrow (inset, below),
known to employ the clever strategy of landing atop a
reed so as to bend it by the force of its weight and more
easily extract seeds from the reed tip. Nests close to the
ground in branches or vine tangles. Sings from a high
perch a one pitched, rapid-fire trill of dry *chip* notes.
Call in flight is a sharp *tseet*, otherwise a high *tsip*.

Habitat

Found in suburban parks and gardens, woodland
edges and clearings; prefers conifers when breeding.

Local Sites

The Chipping Sparrow breeds statewide but leaves
most areas in winter.

FIELD NOTES Once Chipping Sparrows head farther
south in October, they are replaced in brushy fields
and woodland edges by American Tree Sparrows,
Spizella arborea (inset: nonbreeding), characterized by a
head striped with rufous and gray and a dark central breast
splotch. Listen for its sharp, high, bell-like *tink* notes.

Year-round | Adult

FIELD SPARROW

Spizella pusilla L 5.6" (15 cm)

FIELD MARKS

Gray face with rufous crown; some with rufous behind eyes

Distinct white eye ring; pink bill

Streaked brown back and wings

Breast and sides gray or buff-colored; belly grayish white

Behavior
Remains low to the ground in fields and open brush, foraging for insects, caterpillars, seeds, and spiders. Will land atop a reed or grass stem in order to bend it down to the ground with its weight and more easily extract seeds. Found singly or in a pair in spring and summer; forms small family groups after breeding; and in larger, mixed-species foraging flocks in winter. Female builds nest of grasses, leaves, and roots on the ground or in a bush low to the ground, often near water. Song is a series of clear, plaintive whistles accelerating into a trill. Call note is a high, sharp *chip*. In flight, listen for the Field Sparrow's high, loud *tseees*.

Habitat
Found in open, brushy woodlands; shrubby, overgrown fields; and in wooded clearings near water.

Local Sites
The Field Sparrow is a common breeder in shrubby fields at low elevations. It is a common migrant along the coast during October.

FIELD NOTES Field Sparrows flourished with the widespread abandonment of farmlands in the early 1900s, which opened up countless acres of ideal nesting habitat. Now that suburbs and successional forests are taking over farmlots, their numbers are declining.

Year-round | Adult

SAVANNAH SPARROW

Passerculus sandwichensis L 5.5" (14 cm)

FIELD MARKS
Yellow or whitish eyebrow

Pale median crown stripe on streaked crown

Dark brown streaked upperparts

White below with brown streaking on chin, breast, and flanks

Behavior
Forages on the ground singly or in a pair for insects, spiders, and seeds in spring and summer. Forms loose flocks in migration and winter that feed primarily on seeds and berries. Sometimes scratches in dirt like a towhee. Nests on the ground in depression concealed by grasses. Song begins with two or three *chip* notes, followed by long buzzy trill and a final *tip*. Common call is a high *tip*. Flight call is a thin, descending *tseew*.

Habitat
The Savannah Sparrow breeds in a variety of open habitats, such as grasslands, farm fields, and pastures.

Local Sites
Breeds and migrates commonly statewide. Look for it along the coast, such as at Gabreski Airport on the east end of Long Island, during fall migration in October.

FIELD NOTES The larger Fox Sparrow, *Passerella iliaca* (inset), appears throughout New York in migration, especially in the spring. Like the Savannah, it remains close to the ground, sometimes foraging like a towhee, but it prefers more densely wooded areas. It is much more rufous overall, and its breast streaking converges into a large central splotch.

Year-round | Adult

SONG SPARROW

Melospiza melodia L 6.3" (16 cm)

FIELD MARKS
Underparts whitish, with streaks
on sides and breast that converge
into a dark breast spot

Streaked brown and gray above;
broad, grayish eyebrow; broad,
dark malar stripe

Long, rounded tail

Behavior
Forages in trees and bushes and on ground for insects,
larvae, seeds, and berries, sometimes scratching ground
to unearth food. Nests on the ground or near it in trees
and bushes. Female broods young while male defends
territory intently, singing from exposed perch and bat-
tling competitors. Perches in the open, belting out its
melodious song, three to four short, clear notes followed by a buzzy *tow-wee*, then a trill. Common call is
a nasal, hollow *chimp*. Flight call is a clear, rising *seeet*.

Habitat
Common in suburban and rural gardens, weedy fields,
dense streamside thickets, and forest edges.

Local Sites
The Song Sparrow breeds throughout the state, and it
is common in migration along the coast, especially in
October and November.

FIELD NOTES The Vesper Sparrow, *Pooecetes gramineus* (inset),
dwells in grasslands and farmlands.
It has a white eye ring, dark ear patch
bordered in white along lower and rear
edges, and white outer tail feathers
that are conspicuous in flight.

Year-round | Adult

WHITE-THROATED SPARROW

Zonotrichia albicollis L 6.8" (17 cm)

FIELD MARKS
Broad eyebrow is yellow in front of eye, white or tan behind

Black lateral crown stripes and eye lines; white throat bordered by gray

Streaked rusty brown above, grayish below

Behavior
Employs double-scratch foraging method, raking leaf litter with backward kick of both feet, keeping head held low and tail pointed up. Also forages in bushes and trees for seeds, tree buds, and insects. Nests close to or on ground, often at forest edges near water. Calls include a sharp *pink* and a drawn out, lisping *tseep*, given in flight. Its song, given year-round, is a thin whistle of one or two single notes then three or four longer notes: *pure sweet Canada Canada Canada*.

Habitat
Winters in woodland undergrowth, brush, and gardens. Breeds primarily in shrubby wetlands.

Local Sites
The White-throated Sparrow breeds widely in the mountains, and is common at lower elevations during migration and in winter. Look for it at any backyard feeder in winter.

FIELD NOTES A migrant and winter visitor to New York is the White-crowned Sparrow, *Zonotrichia leucophrys* (inset). With similar habitat and behavioral characteristics as the White-throated, the White-crowned is distinguished by its lack of yellow in front of the eye and its grayish throat, not as clearly defined on its breast.

Year-round | Adult male "Slate-colored"

DARK-EYED JUNCO

Junco hyemalis L 6.3" (16 cm)

FIELD MARKS

Dark gray hood and upperparts
on male, brownish on female

White outer tail feathers in flight

White belly and undertail coverts

Pale pinkish bill

Juvenile streaked brown overall

Behavior

Forages by scratching on ground to expose food and by gleaning seeds, grain, berries, insects, caterpillars, and fruit from vegetation. Occasionally gives chase to a flying insect. Forms flocks in winter, when males may stay farther north or at greater elevations than immatures and females. Nests on or close to ground, sheltered by a bush or in a cavity such as a tree root. Song, given year-round, is a short, musical trill on one pitch. Calls include a sharp *dit,* and a rapid twittering in flight.

Habitat

Winters in a wide variety of habitats, especially patchy wooded areas and including backyard feeding stations. Breeds in high-elevation mixed woodlands.

Local Sites

The Dark-eyed Junco is a widespread breeder, primarily at high elevations. Look for it in Treeman State Park at Ithaca. It can hardly be missed in the winter at any backyard feeder.

FIELD NOTES Though widely scattered geographically and fairly different in their field marks, 12 subspecies of Dark-eyed Junco are recognized by the American Ornithologists' Union. A western form, the "Oregon Junco," is an accidental vagrant rarely seen at feeding stations in New York in winter. It shows a black or dark hood, a reddish brown back, a gray rump, and a white belly.

Year-round | Adult male

NORTHERN CARDINAL

Cardinalis cardinalis L 8.8" (22 cm)

FIELD MARKS

Male is red overall; black on face

Female is buffy brown tinged with red on wings, crest, and tail

Large, conspicuous crest

Cone-shaped, reddish bill; blackish on juvenile

Behavior

Generally seen alone or in a pair in summer; in small groups in winter. Forages on the ground or low in shrubs for insects, seeds, leaf buds, berries, and fruit. Territorially aggressive, attacks not only other birds, but also itself, reflected in windows, rear-view mirrors, and chrome surfaces. Nests in forks of trees and bushes, or in tangles of twigs and vines. Call is a sharp, somewhat metallic *chip*. Sings a variety of melodious songs year-round, including a *cue cue cue,* a *cheer cheer cheer,* and a *purty purty purty*. Listen for courtship duets in spring.

Habitat

Found in gardens and parks, woodland edges, stream-side thickets, and practically any environment that provides thick, brushy cover. The cardinal has adapted so well to landscaped yards and backyard feeders that it continues to expand its range northward into Canada.

Local Sites

These birds are a year-round delight in backyards, parks, and every other habitat throughout the state except the highest mountaintops.

FIELD NOTES Cardinals may appear sleek and streamlined in summer and plumper in winter. This is because, as with many birds, they fluff out their body feathers in colder months in order to create pockets of air that conserve body heat.

Breeding | Adult male

ROSE-BREASTED GROSBEAK

Pheucticus ludovicianus L 8" (20 cm)

FIELD MARKS
Breeding male has black hood
and upperparts, rose red breast
and wing linings, and white underparts

Female brownish above with
white eyebrow and whitish,
streaked underparts

Behavior
Forages in trees and shrubs for insects, caterpillars,
seeds, fruit, and berries. Occasionally hovers to pick
food off tips of branches. Forms flocks in migration
and winter. Courtship display consists of male and
female rubbing bills. Nests in vines, shrubs, or low in
trees. Male sings almost constantly a robinlike series of
warbled phrases. Call is a sharp *eek*.

Habitat
Prefers second-growth deciduous woodlands, but also
found in wooded swamps and some suburban parks.

Local Sites
The Rose-breasted Grosbeak is a widespread breeder,
but it is most easily found during migration in May
and September.

FIELD NOTES The female Rose-breasted Grosbeak (inset), with
its brownish streaked plumage, is easily distinguished from the
adult male, but it can be difficult to tell apart
from an immature male. The first-fall male is
also brownish and streaked above, but has a
buffier breast than the female and may show
some pink. An immature male will also sing,
unlike the female.

Breeding | Adult male

INDIGO BUNTING

Passerina cyanea L 5.5" (14 cm)

FIELD MARKS

Breeding male deep blue overall, darker on head; blackish wings

Female is brownish, with diffuse streaking on breast and flanks and a bluish tail

Fall male has varied amount of brown on back, breast, and lores

Behavior

Forages for insects and larvae from ground level to canopy in spring and summer, switching to a seed and berry diet in the fall. Uses heavy conical bill to crack or hull seeds. Forms mixed-species flocks in migration and winter. Nests in shrubs or low in trees, using weeds, bark, grass, and leaves. Territorially aggressive males will often chase away other males. Call is a dry, metallic *pik*. Sings from high perch a series of varied phrases, usually doubled. Second-year males appear to learn songs from competing males, not from parents.

Habitat

Prefers forest edges and bushy transition zones between fields or clearcuts and second-growth woodlands.

Local Sites

The handsome male Indigo Bunting is a familiar sight along the edges of brushy fields across the state, and it is easily found during migration in September along the coast.

FIELD NOTES The female Indigo Bunting (inset), with her brown back, buffy wing bars, and slightly streaked undersides tends to resemble a sparrow if seen alone. Look for her bluish tail, bicolored bill, and unstreaked head and back to tell her apart from sparrows.

Breeding | Adult male

BOBOLINK

Dolichonyx oryzivorus L 7" (18 cm)

FIELD MARKS

Breeding male is mostly black
with yellowish hindneck and white
scapulars and rump

Female is buffy overall with dark
streaks on head, back, and sides

Fall birds resemble female except
show rich yellow-buff below

Behavior

Typically feeds during the day on insects, caterpillars,
grasses, seeds, and grains. Has been observed feeding at
night in agricultural fields while in migration. Flocks
may number in the thousands in migration. Nests on
the ground in tall grasses or weeds. Male arrives first on
breeding grounds to stake out territory and engage in
flight displays while singing his loud, bubbling, eponymous song *bob-o-link bob-o-link blink blank blink*. Call
is a loud, sharp *pink*.

Habitat

Found in hayfields, weedy meadows, and open grasslands. Winters as far south as Argentina.

Local Sites

The beautiful flight song of the Bobolink can be heard
in pasturelands in much of the state, especially during
late May and June. This species is a common
fall migrant along the coast, especially numerous during September.

FIELD NOTES The female Bobolink (inset) and fall
male show streaking similar to a sparrow's, but
are in general a warmer buff below. Some males
do not actually molt into this plumage until they are
in the middle of migration. Note as well the Bobolink's
sharply pointed tail feathers.

Year-round | Adult male

RED-WINGED BLACKBIRD

Agelaius phoeniceus L 8.8" (22 cm)

FIELD MARKS

Male is glossy black with bright red shoulder patches broadly edged in buffy yellow

Females densely streaked overall

Pointed black bill

Wings slightly rounded at tips

Behavior

Runs and hops while foraging for insects, seeds, and grains in pastures and open fields. Male reveals red shoulder patches when he sings from a perch, often atop a cattail or tall weed stalk. Territorially aggressive, a male's social status is dependent on the amount of red he displays. Nests colonially in cattails, bushes, or dense grass near water. Song is a hoarse, gurgling *konk-la-reee*, ending in a trill. Call is a low *chuk* note.

Habitat

Breeds mainly in freshwater marshes and wet fields with thick vegetation. During winter, flocks forage in wooded swamps and farm fields.

Local Sites

The Red-winged Blackbird is a common breeder and migrant throughout the state, especially easy to find along the coast in November.

FIELD NOTES Usually less visible within large flocks of singing males, the female Red-winged (inset) is streaked dark brown above and has dusky white underparts heavily streaked with dark brown. In winter a whole flock may be found containing only females.

Year-round | Adult

EASTERN MEADOWLARK

Sturnella magna   L 9.5" (24 cm)

FIELD MARKS

Yellow below, with black V-shaped
breast band, obscured in winter

Black-and-whitish striped crown
with yellow supraloral area

Brown above, streaked with black

White outer tail feathers

Behavior

Flicks tail open and shut while foraging on the ground.
Feeds mainly on insects during spring and summer,
seeds and grain in fall and winter. Forms small flocks in
fall and winter. Female constructs a domed nest on the
ground, often woven into the surrounding live grasses.
Male known to brood while female starts second nest.
Often perches on fence posts or telephone poles to sing
three to five (and sometimes more) loud, descending
whistles: *tsweee-tsweee-TSWEEEOOO*. Calls include
a buzzy *dzert*, a high-pitched chatter, and a whistled
weeet in flight.

Habitat

Prefers the open space offered by grasslands, pastures,
meadows, farm fields, and large lawns.

Local Sites

In early April the Eastern Meadowlark is a common
migrant along the Lake Ontario shoreline, especially
at Derby Hill and Braddock Bay.

FIELD NOTES Though its breeding range has been advancing
northward due to the widespread clearing of forests, the Eastern
Meadowlark population has been slowly declining in the eastern
states during the past few decades as it loses suitable habitat to
suburban sprawl.

Year-round | Adult male

COMMON GRACKLE

Quiscalus quiscula L 12.6" (32 cm)

FIELD MARKS

Plumage appears all black; in good light, males show glossy purplish blue head, neck, breast

Long, wedge-shaped tail

Pale yellow eyes

Pointed beak

Behavior

Rarely seen outside of a flock in winter, this grackle moves to large, noisy, communal roosts in the evening. During the day, mainly seen on the ground in a group, feeding on insects, spiders, grubs, and earthworms. Also wades into shallow water to forage for minnows and crayfish. Known to feast on eggs and baby birds. Courtship display consists of male puffing out shoulder feathers to make a collar, drooping his wings, and singing. These birds produce sounds like ripping cloth or cracking twigs. Call note is a loud *chuck*.

Habitat

Prefers open spaces provided by farm fields, pastures, marshes, and suburban yards; requires wooded areas, especially conifers, for nesting and roosting.

Local Sites

An abundant breeder in the state. In a spectacular spring migration in late March and April, tens of thousands move north along the Lake Ontario shoreline.

FIELD NOTES The closely related Boat-tailed Grackle, *Quiscalus major* (inset), a resident of coastal saltmarshes, is larger than the Common Grackle and has duller, brownish eyes. Look for its keel-shaped tail on Long Island and Staten Island.

Year-round | Adult male

BROWN-HEADED COWBIRD

Molothrus ater L 7.5" (19 cm)

FIELD MARKS

Male's brown head contrasts with metallic black body

Female gray-brown above, paler below with a whitish throat

Short, dark, pointed bill

Juvenile streaked below

Behavior

Often forages on the ground among cattle, feeding on insects flushed by the grazing herd. Also feeds heavily on seeds and grain. Generally cocks its tail up while feeding. A nest parasite, it will wander for many miles to lay its eggs in the nests of other species, leaving the responsibilities of feeding and fledging of young to the host birds. Primary song is a series of liquid, purring gurgles followed by a high whistle: *bub ko lum tseeee.* Call is a soft *kek.* Females also give a dry chatter, while males emit a modulated whistle in flight.

Habitat

Found in open areas such as farmlands, pastures, forest edges, and lawns. Also seen around human habitation.

Local Sites

The Brown-headed Cowbird breeds throughout the state in virtually every city, town, field, and farm. Large flocks migrate and spend the winter with blackbirds and grackles on farmlands and other open areas.

FIELD NOTES The Brown-headed Cowbird flourishes in most of North America, adapting to newly cleared lands and exposing new songbirds—now more than 200 species—to its parasitic brooding habit. The female Brown-headed Cowbird lays up to 40 eggs a season in the nests of host birds, leaving the task of raising her young to the host species.

Year-round | Adult male

BALTIMORE ORIOLE

Icterus galbula L 8.3" (21 cm)

FIELD MARKS

Male has black hood and back; bright orange rump and underparts; large orange patches on tail

Female is olive-brown above, orange below, with some black on head and throat

Black wings with white edging

Behavior
Mainly eats caterpillars, but will feed as well on other insects, berries, fruit, even flower nectar. Forages high in bushes and trees. Male bows to female, with wings and tail spread, during courtship. Suspends its bag-shaped nest near the tip of a tree branch about 30 feet up, an adaptation designed to deter egg-eating snakes and mammals. Calls include a whistled *hew-li* and a dry chatter. Song is a variable series of sweet, musical whistles.

Habitat
Breeds in deciduous woodlands and wooded suburbs. In migration, found wherever there are tall trees.

Local Sites
The Baltimore Oriole breeds in woodlands throughout the state, and it is easily found in May along the Lake Ontario shoreline and in September along the coast.

FIELD NOTES Sharing much of the same breeding grounds as the Baltimore Oriole, the Orchard Oriole, *Icterus spurius*, spends most of its time in open woodlands, farmlands, and orchards. The male (inset, bottom) has a black hood and chestnut underparts. The female (inset, top) is olive above and yellow below with dusky wings.

Year-round | Adult male

HOUSE FINCH

Carpodacus mexicanus L 6" (15 cm)

FIELD MARKS

Male's forehead, bib, and rump are typically red, but can be orange or, occasionally, yellow

Brown streaked back, pale belly, streaked flanks

Female streaked dusky brown on entire body

Behavior

Forages on the ground in fields and suburban yards primarily for seeds, sometimes for insects or fruit. Often visits backyard feeders. Seen in large mixed-species flocks during winter. Flies in undulating pattern, during which squared-off tail is evident. Builds cup-like nest on buildings, in shrubs or trees, or on the ground. Male sings a lively, high-pitched song consisting of varied three-note phrases, usually ending in a nasal *wheeer.* Most common call is a whistled *wheat.*

Habitat

Adaptable to varied habitats, these birds are found abundantly in shrubby areas near human habitation, including urban and suburban parks.

Local Sites

Ubiquitous breeders in every habitat, including densely populated urban areas, House Finches are among the most common visitors to backyard feeders.

FIELD NOTES The Purple Finch, *Carpodacus purpureus,* is not purple but rose-red on the adult male (inset, bottom). The female (inset, top) is gray-brown above and heavily streaked below, with a bolder face pattern and a more deeply notched tail than the House Finch. Look for both species in winter at bird feeding stations throughout the state.

Breeding | Adult male

AMERICAN GOLDFINCH

Carduelis tristis L 5" (13 cm)

FIELD MARKS

Breeding male is bright yellow with black cap; female and winter male duller overall, lacking cap

Black wings with white bars

Black-and-white tail; white undertail coverts

Behavior

Gregarious and active. Large winter flocks may include several other species. Typical goldfinch diet, mostly seeds, is the most vegetarian of any North American bird, though the goldfinch does sometimes eat insects. During courtship, male performs exaggerated, undulating aerial maneuvers, and often feeds the incubating female. Nests at forest edges or in old fields, often late in summer after thistles have bloomed so they can be used as nest lining and seeds as food for young. Song is a lively series of trills, twitters, and *swee* notes. Calls include a distinctive *per-chik-o-ree*, and a descending *ti-di-di-di*, given mainly in flight.

Habitat

Found in weedy fields, open woodlands, and anywhere rich in thistles and sunflowers.

Local Sites

These birds are common year-round in city parks, suburbs, and farm fields with scattered trees, everywhere in the state except the thickest forests.

FIELD NOTES The nonbreeding male goldfinch (inset) loses his black cap except for a spot just above the bill and molts into much drabber yellowish brown plumage. The nonbreeding female is similar, but an even drabber grayish overall.

Breeding | Adult male

HOUSE SPARROW

Passer domesticus L 6.3" (16 cm)

FIELD MARKS

Breeding male has black bill, bib, and lores; chestnut eye stripes, nape, back, and shoulders

Winter male less patterned

Female has brown back, streaked with black; buffy eyestripe; and unstreaked grayish breast

Behavior
Abundant and gregarious. Hops around, feeding on grain, seeds, and shoots, or seeks out bird feeders for sunflower seeds and millet. In urban areas, begs for food from humans and will clean up any crumbs left behind. In spring and summer, multiple suitors will chase a possible mate in high-speed aerial pursuit. Females choose mate mostly according to song display. Nests in any sheltered cavity; often usurping it, then vigorously defending it, from other species. Singing males give persistent *chirp* notes. Calls are variable.

Habitat
Found in close proximity to humans. Can be seen in urban and suburban areas and in rural landscapes inhabited by humans and livestock.

Local Sites
From big-city streets to isolated farms, these abundant breeders are found everywhere except in the heavily forested mountains.

FIELD NOTES Also known as the English Sparrow, the House Sparrow was first introduced into New York City in 1851 in an effort control insect pests. It has since spread across the continent to become one of the most successful bird species in North America, to the detriment of many native species. Ironically, its numbers are declining precipitously in its native England.

Color categories reflect the overall colors of a species, not just the head color. Where sexes or ages differ, we typically show the most colorful plumage.

Mostly Black

 Double-crested Cormorant, 57

Turkey Vulture, 67

American Coot, 83

Chimney Swift, 121

American Crow, 153

European Starling, 189

Red-winged Blackbird, 247

Common Grackle, 251

Brown-headed Cowbird, 253

Mostly Black and White

Ring-necked Duck, 35

Greater Scaup, 37

Bufflehead, 39

Common Goldeneye, 41

 Hooded Merganser, 43

 Black-crowned Night-Heron, 65

Great Black-backed Gull, 101

Red-bellied Woodpecker, 127

Yellow-bellied Sapsucker, 129

Downy Woodpecker, 131

Pileated Woodpecker, 135

Eastern Kingbird, 143

Black-capped Chickadee, 165

Yellow-rumped Warbler, 203

Black-and-white Warbler, 211

Eastern Towhee, 225

Rose-breasted Grosbeak, 241

 Bobolink, 245

Mostly Blue

 Belted Kingfisher, 125

 Blue Jay, 151

 Purple Martin, 157

 Tree Swallow, 159

Mostly Gray

Mostly Greenish

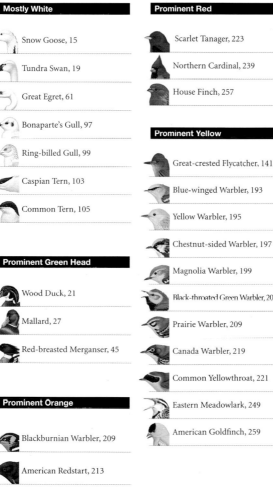

The first entry page number for each species is listed in **boldface** type and refers to the text page opposite the illustration.

A check-off box is provided next to each common-name entry so that you can use this index as a checklist of the species you have identified.

ACKNOWLEDGMENTS

The Book Division would like to thank the following people for their guidance and contribution in creating the *National Geographic Field Guide to Birds: New York.*

Cortez C. Austin, Jr.:
Cortez Austin is a wildlife photographer specializing in North American and tropical birds. An ardent conservationist, he has donated images, given lectures, and written book reviews for conservation organizations. In addition he has published numerous articles and photographs in magazines, field guides, and other books.

Richard Crossley:
Richard Crossley is an Englishman obsessed by birding since age 10. He traveled the world studying birds but fell in love with Cape May while pioneering the identification of overhead warbler migration in 1985. He is co-author of *The Shorebird Guide,* due in Spring 2006.

Bates Littlehales:
A National Geographic photographer for more than 30 years covering myriad subjects around the globe, Bates Littlehales continues to specialize in photographing birds and is an expert in capturing their beauty and ephemeral nature. Bates is co-author of the *National Geographic Photographic Field Guide: Birds* and a contributor to the *National Geographic Reference Atlas to the Birds of North America.*

Robert Royse:
Robert Royse is a professional oboe and English horn player, and is a member of the Columbus Symphony Orchestra. In his spare time, he is an active birder and bird photographer. His bird photographs have been published extensively in books and magazines.

Brian E. Small:
Brian E. Small is a full-time professional wildlife photographer specializing in birds. In addition, he has been a regular columnist and Advisory Board member for *WildBird* magazine for the past 10 years. An avid naturalist and enthusiastic birder, Brian is currently the Photo Editor for the American Birding Association's *Birding* magazine. You can see additional images at www.briansmallphoto.com.

Tom Vezo:
Tom Vezo is an award-winning wildlife photographer who has been widely published in the U.S. and Europe. He is a contributor to the *National Geographic Reference Atlas to the Birds of North America* and the *National Geographic Complete Birds of North America.* Please visit Tom at his website www.tomvezo.com.

Photographs

Cortez C. Austin, Jr.: 20, 58, 84, 162, 190, 248. **Tom Brakefield/CORBIS:** 48. **Richard Crossley:** 94, 182. **Mike Danzenbaker:** 120. **Bates Littlehales:** 116, 212. **Alan Murphy:** 56, 254. **Robert Royse:** 2, 44, 104, 136, 146, 178, 206, 216, 218, 222, 224. **Rulon E. Simmons:** 68, 250. **Brian E. Small:** 32, 34, 40, 42, 60, 66, 70, 88, 90, 92, 106, 108, 110, 118, 124, 142, 144, 148, 154, 160, 170, 176, 180, 184, 186, 188, 192, 194, 198, 200, 204, 210, 220, 226, 228, 230, 232, 234, 238, 242, 258. **Tom Vezo:** Cover, 14, 16, 18, 22, 24, 26, 28, 30, 36, 38, 46, 50, 52, 24, 62, 64, 72, 74, 76, 78, 80, 82, 86, 96, 98, 100, 102, 112, 114, 126, 128, 130, 132, 134, 138, 140, 150, 152, 156, 158, 164, 166, 168, 172, 174, 202, 214, 236, 240, 244, 246, 252, 256, 260. **T. J. Ulrich/VIREO:** 122, 196.

Artwork

Jonathan Alderfer: 10 (bottom), 95. **David Beadle:** 9, 137, 147. **Peter Burke:** 221, 223, 225, 255. **Marc R. Hanson:** 83. **Cynthia J. House:** 15, 17, 19, 21, 25, 27, 31, 33, 35, 37, 39, 41, 43, 45. H. **Jon Janosik:** 55. **Donald L. Malick:** 71, 73, 81, 115, 117, 127, 131. **Killian Mullarney:** 93. **John P. O'Neill:** 165. **David Quinn:** 53. **Kent Pendleton:** 49. **Diane Pierce:** 10 (top), 61, 227, 231, 235, 241, 243, 257, 259. **John C. Pitcher:** 85, 87, 89, 91. H. **Douglas Pratt:** 107, 111, 139, 161, 163, 169, 173, 175, 185, 193, 195, 197, 201, 203, 213, 217, 247, 251. **Chuck Ripper:** 119. **N. John Schmitt:** 75, 233. **Thomas R. Schultz:** 10 (middle), 97, 99, 101, 105, 179, 181, 219, 244.

NATIONAL GEOGRAPHIC
FIELD GUIDE TO BIRDS:
NEW YORK

Edited by Jonathan Alderfer

**Published by
the National Geographic Society**

John M. Fahey, Jr.,
President and Chief Executive Officer

Gilbert M. Grosvenor,
Chairman of the Board

Nina D. Hoffman,
*Executive Vice President;
President, Books & School Publishing*

Prepared by the Book Division

Kevin Mulroy,
Senior Vice President and Publisher

Kristin Hanneman, *Illustrations Director*

Marianne R. Koszorus, *Design Director*

Carl Mehler, *Director of Maps*

Barbara Brownell Grogan,
Executive Editor

Staff for this Book

Barbara Levitt, *Editor*

Kate Griffin, *Illustrations Editor*

Alexandra Littlehales, *Designer*

Carol Norton, *Series Art Director*

Suzanne Poole, *Text Editor*

Teresa Tate, *Illustrations Specialist*

Abby Leopold, *Illustrations Coordinator*

Brian Sullivan, *Map Research*

Matt Chwastyk, Sven M. Dolling,
Map Production

Michael Greninger, *Editorial Assitant*

Rick Wain, *Production Project Manager*

Manufacturing and Quality Control

Christopher A. Liedel,
Chief Financial Officer

Phillip L. Schlosser, *Vice President*

John T. Dunn, *Technical Director*

**Library of Congress
Cataloging-in-Publication Data**

Available upon request

ISBN-10: 0-7922-5564-X

ISBN-13: 978-0-7922-5564-2